D0195385

Table of Contents

Bringing  *Sundance*
Home

THE REAL SUNDANCE
MY GREAT GRANDFATHER

Jerry Nickle
as told by C. J. Del Barto

List of Illustrations

Preface

When I was a mere boy, like most children, I was fascinated with cowboys: Roy Rogers, Whip Wilson, Gene Autry, Wild Bill Hickok, Wyatt Earp, and the like. They were great for my young soul.

I was often decked out with a cowboy hat, chaps, and boots, using a broomstick as a horse with my pearl-handled cap pistol blazing away.

At what age I don't remember, but I was told stories about my great grandfather who was supposedly connected with outlaws and was possibly one himself. It blew me away and tore my socks off that I might have my very own outlaw relative!

As years passed, while most kids my age followed the more modern comic book heroes, I clung to being a cowboy. It suited me then and it more than suits me now.

Even though I don't walk around with my holster and Colt .45 strapped to my hip or run someone down itching for a gunfight because they cut me off in traffic, riding my horse across the open plains or along a mountainside with the wind in my face and the scent of nature all around reminds me how I always wanted to be a cowboy.

About a million years went by, but I always had in the back of my mind to see what I could find out about my great grandfather. Someday... one day...pretty soon...Yep, I'm going to get to it and do some research.

In 2004, after being full of wonder for so long, I finally took the plunge and started extensively researching his background and all that pertained to him. It didn't matter what I might find; I wanted to uncover all there was to know about my relative, "the outlaw."

Everyone dies, the sun rises in the east, and there are billions of stars in the universe. These truths cannot be refuted. I will offer you a new truth. While it may not be earth shattering, it is history changing. It has impacted me and my family and will impact many more once all the facts are known.

FACT: My great grandfather, William "Bill" Henry Long, was the gun-slinging outlaw known as the Sundance Kid, the close friend and cohort of Butch Cassidy.

FACT: Butch Cassidy and the Sundance Kid did not die in Bolivia in 1908 as many books, news articles, and the Academy Award winning movie Butch Cassidy and the Sundance Kid allege. They came home to America, settled in the West, and died many years later as senior citizens.

FACT: Harry Alonzo Longabaugh was one of the many aliases Bill Long used and identities he stole, which is why Longabaugh—who was a real person—is often misidentified as the Sundance Kid.

FACT: William Henry Long was framed as a horse thief and rail-roaded into serving eighteen months in the Sundance, Wyoming, jail where he got his distinctive nickname.

FACT: Contrary to the movie's depiction that he led a freewheeling, carefree lifestyle with girlfriend Etta Place, Sundance had a wife and eight children at his home in Fremont, Utah.

FACT: There so many twists, turns, hills, and valleys in this story that you're going to need a road map and will no doubt ask, Is this for real? The answer is emphatically and factually, yes!

If your reaction was anything like mine, you're probably picking your jaw up from the floor about now. Then again, you might be hee-hawing, thinking it's a bunch of baloney, to put it politely. But get to know the story of my great grandfather Bill Long first before making a final judgment.

Preface

Between the excellent 1969 movie, the many books, and thousands of articles it's virtually impossible to separate the Sundance Kid from Butch Cassidy and vice versa so it's necessary to include both in this story.

Each man had his own distinctive personality. Butch was outgoing and had the reputation of having never killed one of God's children. Sundance, on the other hand, was more somber and aloof and there's no doubt he ushered more than a few men to their graves. Both men had the reputation of being very generous with their ill-gotten money, and were considered by many to be the Robin Hoods of their time.

It might very well be that they knew firsthand what it felt like to be poor in the hard times of the early west and wanted to help those who couldn't help themselves. I believe they gave as we do today for the same reason: we have and some don't.

Not all people are Robin Hoods, but most civilized human beings have a compassion that leads us to help others and gives us a warm feeling of satisfaction knowing we helped.

Yes, they robbed. Yes, men died in the process. Yes, they flouted the law. Yes, they bribed lawmen. Yet, they were so endearing in the movie that we all want more.

This book highlights over 125 years of misinformation, exaggerations, and outright inaccuracies and reveals who in fact was the real Sundance Kid, why he turned to banditry, and how he and Butch got to be the most successful outlaws of the American West and of that other continent, just down the road a piece, South America.

Sit back and allow me to unfold a treasure trove of interesting, entertaining, and factual exploits of my great-grandfather, the Sundance Kid.

~ **Jerry Nickle**

Foreword

Jerry Nickle has invested a great deal of time trying to find a connection, any connection, the connection, to his great-grandfather's past as a western outlaw in the 1880s through the early 1900s. If he was a bandit, with whom did he ride or did he ride alone? Was he famous or just an ordinary, low-key outlaw?

In 2004, Jerry stumbled on a curiously dramatic coincidence: a single picture that is about 132 years old provided to him by a cousin. Seeing it was far more than an ah ha moment. Could it be? It might be. Looks like him!

He had seen a picture years before of some decked out outlaw cowboys taken in Fort Worth, Texas, that had been floating around since 1900. One of the outlaws looked very similar to a picture of his great-grandfather he had just seen. He couldn't push his curiosity aside.

Discoveries are usually a direct result of someone posing a question. Jerry went about asking a gazillion questions over the years, trying to get an answer and then: Eureka!

He put together a massive puzzle with a herd of missing pieces that answered his questions about whether his great grandfather was an outlaw and whom he rode with. The answer surpassed his wildest expectations.

I admire that Jerry doggedly followed his dream as a young boy to finally nail down the wonderful story he is sharing with you now. I loved every bit of it. I hope you will too.

I was fortunate enough to be in the loop the past few years of his search and caught the bug he carried. I hope once you read this story, you will have gotten bugged too.

~ **C.J. Del Barto**

1
CHAPTER

It Had To Start Somewhere

P robably 99.99 percent of those reading this book did not realize there was a mystery surrounding the Sundance Kid's real identity, which was exactly the way he wanted it. Like most outlaws of his day, the Kid used aliases. It's not a good idea to use your real name when you're in bandit mode, stealing and robbing. But by intentionally planting those seeds of disinformation back then, he misled me and generations of others who thought they knew who the Sundance Kid really was.

His outlaw cohorts, including Butch Cassidy, never gave Sundance up to the law, even when they themselves got caught. Likewise, Sundance's casual friends on the Outlaw Trail never tried to collect any of the many rewards offered for him either.

Whether such loyalty was forged by an outlaw code or the simple fear that Sundance would put a bullet between their eyes, those around the Kid helped keep his true identity a mystery that has endured since Sundance acquired his nickname more than 125 years ago in 1887.

The most unusual circumstance of this genealogical journey of discovery is that the general public had no idea that there was a mystery at all. Is that Sundance's genius, luck, or both?

I feel comfortable that his actions were based on a desire to defend his family's name, avoid embarrassment, and prevent another trip to prison, which would be for a much longer stint than before. Mostly, I suspect his biggest reason for using aliases was to protect his wife, children, and grandchildren from not just his criminality but his infidelity as well.

If his family knew him as Sundance, then they would also know of his beautiful, young girlfriend, Etta Place, who often travelled with him. That would have surely hurt his true love Luzernia and their children.

It's not that far-fetched. Parents do what they need to do and few fathers would want their family to know that he caroused with other women and lived a life of banditry as an outlaw gunslinger and killer.

I don't condone his crimes. I wish only to set the record straight as to who he really was and to shed some light on the family man side of Sundance who took care of six step-children and two biological children as a caring father, husband, and later as a grandfather.

Most outlaws of the Old West did not ply their trade full time; it was more like a great high paying part-time position. The average income per household back then was about $50 a month at the most. Imagine getting a lump sum of a $1000 or more for a few days' work.

They would rob a train or a bank, steal a few head of cattle or horses and some of those with families used their ill-gotten money to pay off bills and care for their children. Other outlaws, bought ranches and quit the outlaw trail. A good many blew their money on gambling, drinking, and brothels.

Most of the time, they would actually get a paying ranch job for several months, making $35 a month, even though their pockets or dirt banks (buried money) were full of loot; they might have the equivalent of three to six years ranch salary in a hole somewhere while working for $35 a month.

That might be why only the careless of them got caught or killed. In essence, they just laid low after the deed was done.

Butch Cassidy's gang was like a revolving door for outlaws; when some members were with their families, others would jump in on a job, make some money, and then go home. It's hard to put a number on the number of men who were involved with just Butch, just Sundance, or Butch and Sundance, but it was more than likely about thirty to forty men—and sometimes women.

Sometimes, if not all the time, some outlaws used Butch and Sundance's name when they robbed a train or bank. All wore masks or disguised themselves by growing beards and dyeing their hair; so it was hard to know who was behind the mask or beard. Because of that Butch and Sundance were given credit for robberies they did not commit.

When I first read Charles Kelly's Butch Cassidy book, *The Outlaw Trail,* and saw my grandfather Jerry Jackson mentioned, [1] I was thrilled and yet disappointed.

Kelly was a close friend of my grandfather and my uncles, and had heard the same stories about William Long I had, most likely even more, but there was no mention of him or his connection to the group of bandits.

On January 17, 1976, the *Deseret News* of Salt Lake City, Utah, published an interview with Lula Parker Betenson, Butch Cassidy's youngest sister, "Outlaw's Sister Sets the Record Straight." A photo caption mentions my uncle:

Perry Jackson of Fremont says his step-granddaddy, Bill Long, carried guns [shown] below, when he rode with Wild Bunch.

This confirmation that great-grandpa Bill rode with Butch came as no surprise to family members but why wasn't he mentioned in any other published material?

In her book, Lula Betenson states Butch visited her in Circleville, Utah, in 1925. I recalled hearing that Butch also visited my grandparents,

Jerry and Chloe Jackson, in Fremont, Utah, around the same time. In addition, Bill and Luzernia's daughter Viola stated that Sundance was in Price, Utah, about the same time Butch was in Circleville. We all knew he was involved with Butch but were unsure how.

When the Butch and Sundance movie came out, I saw it hoping to get a clue how William Long fit into the Wild Bunch gang but left very disappointed because there was no mention of him at all.

At a family reunion in the summer of 2004, I was shown an original picture of William Long when he was about 21 years old. His amazing likeness to Sundance in the famous *Fort Worth Five* picture had smoke billowing from my ears. I had to prove it, one way or the other, if only to satisfy my own curiosity.

FORT WORTH FIVE

Front Row: Sundance Kid Ben Kilpatrick Butch Cassidy
Back: Will Carver Harvey Logan

William (Bill) Henry Long
(Denver Public Library)

The Sundance Kid.

I started compiling any and all documents, information, and stories from family members. Everything pointed to one conclusion: William Henry Long was Harry Longabaugh, the Sundance Kid.

I created a website (www. sundancekidhenrylong.com) to post my ideas for others to evaluate, provide more details, and assist in proving or disproving my theory. The website had my email address (jnickle364@yahoo.com) where readers contacted me. I met some very knowledgeable people that helped me including many relatives that I had never met before. I am hoping more people with new information will contact me and I will add to or edit this book.

All the available records state that Harry Longabaugh was the Sundance Kid. I surmised William Long was really Harry Longabaugh and just used the Long name when he was with his family. But it was actually the other way around. William used Harry's name as his alias when he rode with Butch Cassidy.

Notes:
1. Charles Kelly, *The Outlaw Trail: A History of Butch Cassidy and His Wild Bunch* (Lincoln, NE: Bison Books, 1996), 22.

2
CHAPTER

Characters' Ancestry

F rom government censuses and other records I've pieced together the Sundance Kid's ancestry.

His great grandparents were Ware Long (1750-1833) and Ann Nancy Sinath Long (1762-1830). Ann was half French and half Cherokee Indian. She and the following generations could speak both French and English. Sundance spoke English with a slight French accent. (One of the descriptions for Sundance identifies him as having Creole type features. Technically he was not Creole because he was not from Louisiana like the Creoles are but he had French/Indian ancestry the same as Louisiana Creoles do.)

William's grandparents were Abner Long (1782-1860) and Sara Sally Stover (1792 - unknown). Abner was born in Purgatory Creek, Virginia, which had a substantial French population at the time.

Sara was born in Henry County, Virginia, the daughter of Henry Stover (1741-1798) and Magdalena Kirstaetter (1741-1797).

Sundance's father was James Long, born in Ohio in 1826, and his mother Ann was born in England in 1830.

The 1850 census shows the James Long family lived in Orion Township, Illinois. For reasons unknown, they moved temporarily to Decatur City, Iowa, but returned to Orion by 1860.

William Henry Long was born February 2, 1861.

Sometime after 1870, the Longs moved west to the Washington Territory. It was a brutal journey and there are many accounts of the hardships and dangers early settlers of the west endured to reach their destinations. One that strikes me profoundly is about Butch Cassidy's grandfather and grandmother and their children, recounted in Lula Parker Betenson's book. The family, which included Butch's father Maximillian, traveled to Utah using a wooden-wheeled handcart the size of a rickshaw instead of a wagon like most other pioneers, so it took them almost four months to get there.

Imagine leaving home with only the bare essentials—a few pieces of clothing, family mementos, pots and pans for cooking. Those who took a covered wagon could bring along a few chickens, a pig, perhaps even a cow. But even then they still had to catch or kill their daily food on the trail.

Wagons were pulled by horses or oxen but the Parkers had to push or pull their handcart over dirt and rocks and potholes, up and down hills, every day for the four month, 2000 mile trek to Utah.

The children, like the adults, had to walk and the family endured the constant anxiety over the possibility of an attack by unfriendly Indians, mountain lions, bears, and wolves.

And that was before they reached the rugged Rocky Mountains, first struggling to climb narrow uphill trails, then navigating steep, downhill slopes on the last leg of the journey all the while trying to keep the packed cart from tumbling over the edge.

Those were the hardy, determined men and women who forged the Western spirit. They could build anything, endure any hardship, and overcome any obstacle. They carved out a new world inside our country and sought to instill the same work ethic and determination in their children.

The next time you're out west in the mountains, look around and imagine yourself carving out a living in that rugged country without modern equipment, no electricity or running water, or the many conveniences we have today. Families like the Parkers deserve nothing less than a big salute.

I don't know all the details of the Long family as they moved from one place to another. Their moves are only documented in the census records.

Once the Longs arrived in Washington, the family settled in an area called Cloverland in what is now the plateau country of Asotin County[1], known for its rolling hills and farms. During their time there, the area was primarily a grain production and cattle ranching area. According to Bill Long's daughter Viola, he left home as a teen to attend a cowboy camp and later worked as a ranch hand.

Ann Long died in 1880 and James remarried Lucy Ann Baldwin a year later. After his father remarried, Bill left home for good.

In 1887, James passed away, and his descendants left Asotin County.

In 1899, Bill's brother Nelson Long was convicted of horse theft in Kittitas County and sentenced to three years in the Washington State Prison at Walla Walla. He was released on December 25, 1901.[2]

Mug Shot of Nelson Long
(Courtesy of Walla Walla Prison Records, Walla Walla, WA.)

James Allred was among those to heed the call of Mormon Church president Brigham Young and brought his wife Elizabeth Warren Allred and their twelve children to Utah.

In the spring of 1851, they established the Allred Settlement in central Utah's Sanpete Valley. Later, the town was called Canal and then eventually renamed Spring City.

In 1854, the Allred's youngest child, Andrew Jackson "Jack" Allred, married Chloe Stevens and started a family. Their daughter Luzernia Allred was born April 27, 1857. In 1872 Chloe died, and in 1873 Jack married Elizabeth Ivie.

Jack and his family lived in Spring City until 1876 when they relocated to the picturesque Rabbit Valley and established a trading post frequented by the local Indians.[3] The valley is fifteen miles long and six miles wide, with the clear Fremont River running through it. Today Rabbit Valley is home to Fremont, Loa, Lyman, and Bicknell and residents and many others say if there is a heaven on earth, it's there.

Allred Point Monument: Loa, Utah
(Author' Collection)

Fremont and Loa Utah
(Courtesy of Brent Nickle)

The Allred family was the first white settlers in the valley, which was the ancestral home to a band of Piute Indians. The Piutes and the Allreds earned each other's mutual respect; so much so that according to records Jack was given the name *Shungitz* and his brother James was given the name *Showitz*.

I suspect both names had a similar meaning to *Shivwits*, which roughly translates to "the people who live in the east or, band of Piutes." It seems they thought enough of the Allred's to call them brother Piutes.

Jack built some adjoining cabins that were used as lodging for travelers, a forerunner to motels. The trading post also served as the first post office for the county. The merchandise sold or traded included bolts of calico, ammunition, nails, and homemade shoes. There was a barrel of salted trout for those that didn't want to catch their own in Spring Creek or the Fremont River. Luzernia made gloves and overalls from buckskin used for trade by local Indians.

Aside from being one of the early pioneers of Wayne County, Utah, it gives me goose bumps to think that if not for Luzernia, my great grandmother, I would not be here today.

The William Morrell family followed the Allreds to Rabbit Valley. William's oldest son, Silas, claimed the first and one of the best homesteads in the valley, with the Fremont River running through part of his land. The modern town of Fremont is located on part of the old Morrell's homestead.

Just months after arriving in the valley, Silas married 19 year- old Luzernia on July 12, 1876 after a whirlwind romance. Their homestead would eventually become the Sundance Kid's home.

William Morrell and his four sons, including Silas, established a sawmill five miles north of town on the Fremont River. Silas split his time working the sawmill and his homestead.

**The Morrell Saw Mill was located in the Trees in Bottom of Canyon
(Courtesy of Brent Nickle)**

Silas and Luzernia had seven children. The eldest was Chloe, my grandmother, who was born March 15, 1878; followed in short order by Warren on December 8, 1879 and Clara on August 1, 1880.

The family lived happily until a tragic accident at the sawmill happened two months after Clara was born.

Ten month old Warren fell into the mill's pond and drowned. The heartbroken parents laid little Warren to rest on a hill overlooking Allred Point so Luzernia could watch over her son as she worked.[4]

It was mostly Luzernia who ran the Allred Trading Post, also known as Jack's Point, so she became acquainted with everyone who stopped by, from local Piute Indians and cattle rustlers to horse thieves and outlaws.

To evade lawmen biting at their heels, outlaws used an ancient Indian trail—now Utah State Highway 24—that took them past Jack's Point and followed the Fremont River to Robbers Roost. From there several trails branched off that led into Telluride and other Colorado mining towns where bandits would sell the cattle and horses they had stolen in Utah.

Jack's Point had the first water for thirsty travelers and their animals after the long climb over the summit from Grass Valley twenty miles to the west. Jack's Point also sold or traded that famed dreaded necessity, whiskey.

Among those Luzernia met was a cattle rustler and horse thief named Tom McCarty. Tom was born in Iowa in 1850, and his parents established a ranch in Grass Valley.[5] Tom's brother Bill was also a cattle rustler and horse thief.

Here's a highly coincidental piece of history: according to Matt Warner's book, *Last of the Bandits Riders,* the McCarty boys were first cousins to William Henry McCarty, also known as William Bonney, better known as Billy the Kid.[6]

In 1884 Luzernia met 18-year-old Robert Leroy Parker "Butch Cassidy" at Jack's Point. Butch was born in Beaver, Utah, on Friday the 13th of April 1866. His parents were Maximillian Parker and Ann Gillies. By 1880 the Parker family included six children with more to come. They decided to leave Beaver and buy a ranch just outside Circleville, Utah.

Money was scarce so Maximillian found work elsewhere and Ann worked at the Marshall ranch twelve miles south of Circleville. It was here that young Robert (Butch) fell under the influence of a cattle rustler named Mike Cassidy. Because of the assumed mentoring by

Cassidy, Butch would later take the name of Cassidy and used it most of his outlaw life.

The Butch part came from the time he worked in a butcher shop in Rock Springs, Wyoming, where patrons referred to him as Butch. Ergo, the name of one of the west's most endearing outlaws took root, Butch Cassidy. [7]

However, in his book, *Last of the Bandit Riders,* Matt Warner says in essence, "He had a gun he nicknamed Butch because it kicked real bad, and he had Butch sit in a wobbly legged chair and had him shoot it; it kicked so hard that it knocked him over, to the laughter of all there," and that's where Matt Warner said the nickname "Butch" came from.

In either case, he was known by Butch Cassidy most of his life, along with ten to twelve other aliases.

Butch left home in 1884 after he was incriminated by two other young Mormon teenagers for stealing some horses. He then headed toward Telluride, Colorado; with the commandeered horses. [8] About 50 miles from home he arrived at the trading post where he met Luzernia, who would later become the wife of his best friend and partner, The Sundance Kid.

Younger Luzernia (Allred-Morrell)
(Authors' Collection)

Granite Ranch Today
(COURTESY OF Brent Nickle)

After 75 more miles, Butch arrived at Robbers Roost, where he turned the horses over to the more experienced horse thief Cap Brown. After they sold the horses in Telluride, [9] Butch spent some time there, and later that summer, he returned to Robbers Roost where he became acquainted with Charlie Gibbons. Gibbons owned the Fair View Ranch and the store and hotel in nearby Hanksville. [10]

Gibbons helped Butch get a job at the nearby Granite Ranch, where rustlers and horse thieves were always welcome. [11] Perhaps the ranch owner bought some of their ill gotten, four-legged booty. While working at the Granite Ranch Butch would have made friends with the shadier cowboys who worked there.

Ann Bassett was also known as Etta Place or at least one of possibly two who used the name. She was born May 25, 1878, in Brown's Park, Colorado, and was the first white child born there.

When Ann's parents Herb and Elizabeth Bassett first arrived in that part of Colorado, the area was called Brown's Hole but Elizabeth found the name offensive and insisted it be called Brown's Park. Apparently, she got her way.

Ann's older sister Josie was born in 1874 before the Bassetts came to Brown's Park. The Bassett family was among the first settlers in the area. Brown's Park is a unique area, with most of its area in Colorado and smaller parts in Wyoming and Utah. The Bassett girls were a big part of Brown's Park history.

Brown's Park was a favorite hideout for bandits and the Bassetts became acquainted with all the outlaws. If authorities were pursuing a bandit from one state he could easily cross over the state line into different jurisdiction just a few miles away.

Butch Cassidy once worked at the Bassett Ranch. It's also possible that Sundance worked there for a short time, but I cannot legitimately place him there. He did, however, know the Bassett girls, to say the least. [12]

Ann Bassett (aka) Etta Place
(Courtesy the Denver Public Library)

In 1877, President Ulysses S. Grant opened the Wallowa Valley of eastern Oregon to be settled by pioneers. Grant demanded that all of the roaming Nez Perce Indians immediately move onto the Lapwai Reservation located in present day Idaho.

Despite the best efforts of Indian Chief Joseph to negotiate these demands, Civil War veteran Brigadier General Oliver O. Howard gave a thirty-day ultimatum with a threat to comply, or else!

The threat got the Indian bands to move away reluctantly, but it also sparked the anger of a group of young Nez Perce warriors. This spark quickly grew into flames, and these young warriors staged murderous raids that targeted settlers along the Snake River of what is currently Asotin County, Washington.

Unfortunately, this is where William Long's family had settled. During this time, a Native American warrior killed one of my great uncles, Frank Long. His father, James Long had the horrifying experience of seeing his dead son atop the horse that carried the burden of his body home.

Grief stricken, James Long told his children that no one could ride that horse. Not necessarily one to obey orders, William rode his dead brother's horse anyway, returning home with the horse all lathered up.

James beat his young son and as a result, William ran away from home to a cowboy camp. When James went to bring William home, the cowboys successfully hid him. He was a mere child fending for himself. It must have been one heck of a beating.

Little is known of William's cowboy life as a teenager, except he worked with his father and at neighboring ranches before leaving home. He once recounted, "I swam across the swift moving Snake River while holding onto the tail of a horse."

Sundance's daughter Viola, wrote the following letter to her nephew, Silas Laverle Morrell in 1937, almost a year after Sundance's death. This letter was the key to uncovering Sundance's genealogy by locating him in United States census records.

The story of my father as near as I know. My father, William Henry Long, left his home when a very small boy, (six years) and went to a cowboy camp. It seems as if grandfather went for him several times, but the cowboys hid him and kept my grandfather from finding him. In later years he met up with a fellow who had a picture of two girls, which my father recognized as his two sisters. My father got this picture. And at the age of about 21 as near as he could remember he came to Utah and latter married my mother and had two girls. I am the oldest and very anxious to locate some of my father's people. My father died last November 27 1936. Sometimes I wonder if his real name was Long, but I think I can see resemblance in the picture. My father never would talk about his people or his past life but very little. I think my grandfather was French and I do remember his saying his father was a cattleman and farmer and lived somewhere near Boise. The record of my father as near as I know my grandfather James Long my Grandmother Ann. Brothers and sisters: Abner killed by Indians and his horse brought his body home, Charles, Frank, William Henry my father, Nelson, Lucy married Jim Moss, Sarah Salina, Mary Mahalia. The names are not in older of ages but I don't know which is the oldest. But the picture which was taken at Lewiston Idaho, J.W. Riggs photographer.[13]

As you can see, she was mostly in the dark about her own father. No doubt Sundance wanted it that way to cover his banditry and womanizing ways.

I need to present what's known about the life of Harry Longabaugh because as previously mentioned; his name was the primary alias that Bill Long used. Longabaugh allowed Sundance to take the fall for him for a stolen horse and pistol.

Harry Alonzo Longabaugh was born in the spring of 1867 in or around Upper Providence Township, Pennsylvania. Longabaugh was listed as a 13-year-old in the 1880 census as a hired servant living with the Wilmer Ralston family in West Vincent, Pennsylvania.

In August 1882, the 15-year-old Harry left home with his cousin George and his family for Durango, Colorado, where they bred and raised horses.

About two years later, George moved his family to Cortez, Colorado, and Harry went with them and stayed until he was about 18 years old. [14] Cortez was a stopover for cattle drives up from Texas, heading northward.

When Longabaugh left Cortez, he headed for the Powder River Basin and obtained work for $35 per month at the Suffolk Cattle Company about thirty miles north of Lusk, Wyoming.

Everett C. Johnson was one of the foremen at the neighboring Powder River Cattle Company ranch that same summer. He and Longabaugh became very good friends, with this friendship lasting many years.

Johnson was sent to Alberta, Canada, in the fall of 1886 to locate a new ranch site for the cattle company. Johnson became a Canadian citizen and remained there the rest of his life. Longabaugh would eventually work for Johnson at various ranches in Canada. [15]

Longabaugh only worked a few days at the Suffolk Ranch before he was fired.

Sam Mather, a co-worker tells the story in a letter he wrote to a friend stating:

Our foreman put Harry to wrangling horses the first week on the roundup: he ended up whipping three other wranglers and came very close to whipping our Dutch cook for calling him Longdoy. He got along fine after that until we got back to the ranch where the sheriff of Lusk arrested him for robbing an old man of $80, but he got away that night. [16]

It looks like Longabaugh was a budding thief at the age of 19. After leaving the Suffolk Ranch, he went to Montana and obtained work at the N Bar N ranch outside of Miles City where he met and worked with Sundance.

It's important to say that in the Old West, you either worked your own settlement, farm, or ranch or you worked for a bigger ranch that could pay you. Top dollar was $35 per month, including board.

Most towns had one general store, one livery stable, one bank, one café/hotel, one saloon, and no convenience stores. Children of the day might receive two to four years of education. Some didn't get any. They were needed to help grow, raise, and harvest their own food, milk the cows, plow the fields, and do whatever else needed doing.

In the Old West of the 1840s through the early 1900s if you put down roots in the early communities, you knew everyone and they knew you based simply on the limited population then. It was more the rule than the exception to actually protect each other and help put up your neighbor's house or barn, share fence mending, or swap a pig for several chickens.

Even today, members of any given church socialize, have associations, join in festivities together, and advance their ideals with others. You can bet the tight-knit Mormons of the early West did the same.

One was always welcome by other church members as he traveled or worked away from his own home.

A note to those who grew up with modern grocery stores that supply our processed meats and vegetables; in the simpler times, you raised your own chickens, pigs, cows and planted seeds for vegetables.

Of course, you had to cut the veggies from the ground and slaughter the cows, chickens, and pigs yourself. The good news is I have never heard it said, nor have I heard firsthand, any veggie squeal when plucked from the ground and cut up for dinner. The bad news, the chickens, pigs, and cows did not go quietly.

Your closest neighbor might be a few miles away since most homesteads were on 160 acres of land. That has the sound of fresh air and silence, doesn't It? By the way, the cost for that land was usually $250.

Make no mistake about it, settlers were a close knit group, unlike today when neighbors rarely socialize together and don't know each other very well. It may have had a lot to do with the inherent dangers of the rugged life they had to endure daily and the circumstances of just getting out west to find their dream.

In those days, there were simply farmers, ranch hands, cowboys, and those that had the Big Ranches and all the money and, there weren't many job prospects in between.

In the United States, the 1860s through the 1890s were the boom years for cattle. Massive herds were driven up from Texas, through New Mexico, Colorado, Utah, and Wyoming to Montana. Where buffalo once roamed by the millions huge herds of cattle now roamed.

Thousands of cowboys, including Sundance and possibly Butch, worked for these ranches; they rode to Texas by horse, picked up the giant herds, and drove the cattle to their destinations in the northwestern states and territories.

Obviously, these cowpunchers became familiar with each town they passed through along the way. It paid to know where the best entertainment was and the saloons that had the worst or most watered down whisky.

It was during this time that one of these towns, Cortez, Colorado, caused Sundance's life to take an unexpected turn.

The cattle barons, as they were called, had a stranglehold on the bulk of the rangeland and water rights for cattle grazing. They resented any smaller cattleman using the public lands to graze their cattle. Any unbranded cattle, including calves that roamed on land they claimed, were branded as their own.

But if the barons' cattle roamed onto a small rancher's land, the barons accused the rancher of stealing the animals and had them arrested. Later, the barons hired several killers to get rid of their competition. If you, or any member of your family, was on the wrong end of the stick, well that was too bad.

The big banks loaned money to the small ranchers for their irrigation, feed, fencing, and other necessities. However, if you had the slightest glitch because of bad weather, market conditions, or any number of reasonable delays in paying them, come on, you know what's coming. They would take the ranchers' homesteads and sell it to the cattle barons for cheap.

The railroads moved cattle from the west to the big cities in the east by the millions. And of course, the cattle barons were their best customers.

As time passed, many new outlaws popped up as cattle rustlers took the barons' cattle, but never the small ranchers' cattle. A baron's bounty was $300 to $500 to kill rustlers. There was also nothing more effective than a good public hanging to deter others from doing what the barons did themselves.

Every business to ever exist originated by finding a void and filling it. Eventually, someone did the math and determined that if trains moved cattle eastward, trains coming back west likely carried large payrolls back to the banks and their clients the cattle barons. Instead of stealing the cattle, they went straight for the money, the trains and banks.

Naturally, the railroad companies and the banks took exception; they hired more killers to eliminate those pesky crooks.

Now the cycle was complete. You steal from me, I steal from you, you try to kill me, I kill you, etc.

Butch was falsely arrested for stealing three horses even though he had a receipt showing he had purchased them. Admittedly, the person he bought them from had stolen the horses. Butch spent 18 months in the state penitentiary in Laramie, Wyoming. [17] The total value of the horses was $75. (Priceless)

Sundance was falsely arrested for stealing a pistol, a horse with a saddle, and a bridle rig. He spent 18 months in the Sundance, Wyoming jail. The total value of the items stolen was less than $80.

In the Old West, justice was often times nonexistent. Because of the greed of the major cattle barons, railroads, and banks Butch and Sundance were imprisoned for crimes they did not commit.

Is it any wonder why good men went bad?

NOTES

1. Asotin County, Washington Tax Records, Office of the Assessor.

2. Washington State Prison Records, Walla Walla, Washington.

3. Anne Snow, *Rainbow Views: A History of Wayne County* (Springville, UT:Art City Pub, 1985) and Allred Family Records.

4.Eldon Morrell, *Ancestry and Descendants of William Wilson Morrell,* Self-Published, 1988. 45

5. Jon M. Skovlin and Donna McDaniel Skovlin, *In Pursuit of the McCartys* (San Diego: Reflections Publishing, 2001), 1-11.

6. Matt Warner and Joyce Warner, *Last of the Bandit Riders, Revisited* (Salt Lake City: Big Moon Traders, 2000), 30, 31.

7. Lula Parker Betenson and Dora Flack. *Butch Cassidy My Brother* (Provo, UT: Brigham Young University Press, 1975), 32-47.

8. Warner, *Last of the Bandit Riders,* 41.

9. Pearl Baker, *The Wild Bunch at Robbers Roost* (New York: Abelard-Schuman, 1965,1971), 18-20.

10. Jerry D. Wells, *Samuel M. and Minnie Z. Lisonbee, Wells, (Prove, Brigham Young University Press),* 14.

11. Kelly, *Outlaw Trail,* 13, 148.

12. Grace McClure, *The Bassett Women* (Ohio: Swallow Press/Ohio Press, 1985), 9-12.

13. Viola Long Ehlers 1937 Letter, in possession o f Sherma Morrell Payton.

14. Donna B. Ernst, Paul D. Earnst, Dan Buck, and Anne Meadows, *The Sundance Kid* (Norman, OK: University of Oklahoma Press), 6-19

15. Simon M. Evans, The *Bar U and Canadian Ranching History, Calgary Alberta:,* University of Canada Press, 2004, And *Big Hill Country,* 317, 318.

16. John B. Thomas Papers of Suffolk Cattle Company,(Laramie: American Heritage Center, University of Wyoming).

17. Richard Patterson, *Butch Cassidy: A Biography* (Lincoln, NE: Bison Books), *65-69.*

3
CHAPTER

William Henry Long

A fter William Long left home for good, he next shows up as a grown man in the fertile grasslands around Miles City, Montana, which was the closest major cattle center to his former home in the Washington Territory. The N Bar N was the biggest ranch in the area and employed over a hundred cowboys.

The Northern Pacific Railroad ran through Miles City and transported cattle by the hundreds of thousands to eastern cities.

In 1886, Sundance was 25 years old. He worked as a ranch hand, drove cattle up from Texas, and was a broncobuster for the NBarN Ranch so of course he was acquainted with all the cowboys that worked there. One of the many ranch hands that Sundance became acquainted with was a younger cowboy named Harry Alonzo Longabaugh.

After the annual fall roundup was finished, most of the cowboys were let go. As best as I can determine, Longabaugh was laid off in early December 1886. Like most other ranch hands, Harry did not own a horse so he hitched a ride with someone heading toward Wyoming and if he found any work at all it was only for room and board.

On February 27, 1887, just outside of Sundance, Wyoming, as Longabaugh was working his way back to Miles City for the spring season, he stole a light gray horse, a saddle, and bridal rig from Alonzo Craven and a pistol from James Wedner at the Triple V Ranch. When Wedner discovered the theft he knew who the thief was, and what he looked like, but he didn't know his name.

On March 15, Wedner traveled to Sundance and filed charges with Sheriff James Ryan. Wedner described Longabaugh as a "smooth faced gray eyed boy." [1] The 20 year-old Longabaugh obviously could not grow a beard yet.

Riding the stolen horse, Longabaugh went to Miles City, where Sheriff Irvine or one of his deputies arrested him on April 8 and sent word to Sheriff Ryan in Sundance that they had the horse thief in custody. Ryan left immediately for Miles City to collect the prisoner [2]

In Miles City on April 12, Ryan and Longabaugh boarded the Northern Pacific Railroad going to St. Paul, Minnesota, nearly 1,000 miles away. That same day the *Daily Yellowstone Journal* published this article:

Sheriff Ryan departed with his prisoner this morning bound for Sundance, Wyoming. The route taken by the sheriff would seem to be a long one: Miles City to St. Paul Minnesota to the railroad terminus in the Black Hills, thence by stage to Sundance, a distance of nearly 2,000 miles. Sundance is less than 300 miles cross county from here

Near Duluth, Minnesota, Longabaugh picked the locks of his restraints and escaped *by* jumping from the moving train while the sheriff was tending to necessities. When Sheriff Ryan discovered his prisoner had escaped he was furious and issued a $250 reward for his capture.

The Spearfish Weekly Register described Ryan as...*looking dejected and grieved because he had gone up to that country of smart rascals after a horse thief and while he was absent for a few moments, Mr. Prisoner mysteriously disappeared.*

On May 11, 1887, the *Daily Yellowstone Journal* published the name of the escaped prisoner as Harry Longabaugh. This was the first time a name was ascribed to the horse thief.

The Crook County Commission of Sundance, Wyoming, had not authorized the train trip. Now Ryan had a huge problem: he'd lost his prisoner and spent a large sum of money transporting Longabaugh by train rather than taking him back by buckboard or stage coach.

When Ryan returned to Sundance empty handed, the commission refused to pay for the train ride and of course, no prisoner meant no reward money, either.

Ryan notified Sheriff Irvine in Miles City that the prisoner escaped and told him there was a reward offered for his capture, and to keep a lookout for him. But Longabaugh wasn't stupid enough to go back to Miles City where he would be recognized and arrested again. Instead, he headed straight to Alberta, Canada, and met up with Everett Johnson, his old friend from Wyoming. Even if American authorities located him, they couldn't do anything about it because they had no jurisdiction in Canada. [3]

NOTES
1. *Sundance Gazette,* March 18, 1887.
2. *Sundance Gazette,* April 8, 1887.
3. Simon M. Evans, *The Bar U,* 72-75.

4

CHAPTER

A Miraculous Identity Switch

tock inspector W. Smith and Deputy Sherriff Eph Davis of Miles City rearrested the alleged horse thief Harry Longabaugh on June 1. But this cowboy was not Longabaugh.

The circumstances of the arrest were unusual. This cowboy was casually riding along a public road with a cowboy friend when he saw the lawmen coming from the other direction. When they were about to pass this innocent cowboy made the usual greeting. In response the lawmen pulled their pistols, arrested the cowboy and took him into custody. If this cowboy was actually Longabaugh, a wanted man, why would he be traveling a public road?

The arrest happened thirty-eight days from when the real Longabaugh escaped from his shackles and jumped off the train. If this second cowboy was Longabaugh that means he made the 2,000-mile trip back with no money and no horse in less than six weeks. It took Sheriff Ryan 11 days riding a train. And why would

Longabaugh return to Miles City the same place where he was previously apprehended?

The real Longabaugh was kept in the Miles City jail for three days before Sheriff Ryan took custody of him so the local lawman knew what he looked like and yet this cowboy they arrested was different. He was 5' 9" tall with dark hair and a mustache. He was also 26 years old with a French accent and Creole type fetures[1] instead of the smooth faced 20 year-old light complected German kid Harry Longabaugh. Hello... anybody home there?

William (Bill) Henry Long
(Authors' Collection)

The second alleged Longabaugh was accused of making his way back through Canada where he stole seven horses; entered Montana where he sold the horses; and then went to the Crow Indian Reservation where he stole a pony. He then allegedly committed a robbery at the FUF Ranch and then stole a horse from both the Beasley and Newman sheep ranches and the George Liscom ranch on the Tongue River. [2]

To cover that distance and commit all those crimes in that short period of time cannot be done. In addition to all that, he apparently managed to completely reverse his appearance to that of an older and darker Harry, all in 38 days.

This is an excerpt from the *Daily Yellowstone Journal* of June 7, 1887.

Tom Irvine considers him one of the most daring and desperate criminals he has ever had to deal with. The stretch of country the thief has covered in a short time and the success of all his planned robberies was almost phenomenal. Deputy Davis and Inspector Smith did a mighty good job when they nailed the Kid without some blood being spilt. He acknowledged himself done up when landed in this jail, and he expresses much admiration for our officers in the way they did the business.

It's not phenomenal it's impossible. All these thefts were credited to Harry Longabaugh since he was the one originally arrested, and rightfully so. But this second prisoner was not Harry Longabaugh it was William Henry Long, a convenient patsy. Here is another interesting load of elephant stuff. The *Daily Yellowstone Journal* published the alleged Longabaugh's statement/confession after the second arrest. Keep in mind William Long had a rudimentary education as did Harry Longabaugh.

I read a very sensational and partly untrue article, which places me before the public not even second to the notorious Jesse James. Admitting that I have done wrong and expecting to be dealt with according to law, and not by false reports from parties who should blush with shame to make them, I ask a little of your space to set my case before the public in a true light. In the first place I have always worked for an honest living, was employed last summer by one of the best outfits in Montana and don't think they can say aught against me, but having got discharged last winter I went to the Black Hills to seek employment which I could not get and was forced to work for my board a month and a half, rather than to beg or steal. I finally started back to the vicinity of Miles City...for spring round up and was arrested at the above named place and charged with having stolen a horse at Sundance, where I was being taken by Sheriff Ryan, whom I escaped from by jumping from the cars, which I judged were running at the rate of 100 miles an hour.

After this my course of outlawry commenced, and I suffered terribly for the want of food in the hope of getting back south without being detected, where I would be looked upon as I always had been, and not as a criminal. Contrary to the statement in the Journal, I deny having stolen any horses in Canada and selling them near Benton or anywhere else up to the time I was captured...nor had I the slightest idea of stealing any horses. I am aware that some of your readers will say my statement should be taken for what it is worth, on account of the hard name which has been forced upon me; never the less it is true. As for my recapture by Deputy Sheriff Davis, all I can say is that he did his work well. [3]

The June 7 *Daily Yellowstone Journal* detailed the real Harry Longabaugh's escape from the train and also identified this second cowboy arrested as Longabaugh instead of who he really was; William Long. This was the catalyst tagging William Long as Harry Longabaugh forever, until now!

Back in Sundance, Sheriff Ryan was informed that Longabaugh had been recaptured. Ryan set off for Miles City to take him into custody and bring him back to Sundance and collect the reward. The June 19, 1887, *Daily Yellowstone Journal* reported:

Sheriff Ryan from Crook County, Wyoming, is here to take charge of Kid Longabaugh. Mr. Ryan will take precautions this time that will tax the ingenuity and hardihood of a slicker chap than the Kid to get away. This time Sheriff Ryan took his prisoner shackled and handcuffed to Sundance by way of the Miles City and Deadwood Stage.

The Sheriff told the prisoner, "He was going to land him or his scalp in the Sundance Jail."

The prisoner warned the Sheriff "that he intended to escape."

An Old Photo of Sundance, Wyoming
(From Internet)

After three days on the road they reached Sundance and the prisoner was put in jail. This innocent cowboy was also identified as Harry Longabaugh in the court records. But his age, which was 26, was recorded correctly.

The July 22, 1887, issue of the *Sundance Gazette* reported:

Harry (Long) and William McCarter tried to escape jail by removing a hinge on the Cell Door while awaiting trial. They were discovered before they could escape.

Court records show that no witnesses were called on behalf of prisoner. On August 5, 1887, Long pleaded not guilty to the three indictments: the horse, the gun, and the saddle rig. His defense attorney coaxed him into pleading guilty to the one indictment for stealing the horse and the other charges were dropped.

When asked if he had anything to say, Long declined to speak. He was sentenced to eighteen months in the Sundance jail.

If he had been allowed to call witnesses, they would have put him at the N Bar N ranch at the time of the horse theft in Sundance and they would have certainly told the court his real name was William Long, and he was not the "smooth faced horse thief Harry Longabaugh" who they knew as well.

The Pinkerton's description for Sundance also matches William Long: 5'9" or 5'10, weighing 170 to 175 pounds, with a medium-dark complexion, black hair, and blue or gray eyes. He had a black mustache or beard, a rather long nose, a slim build, and Grecian features. In the book *Atlas of Wyoming Outlaws,* the description is virtually the same except it states he had Creole features. Grecian and Creole features are similar.

The minutes from the October 6, 1887, meeting of the Crook County Commission show a bill for $250 from Sheriff Ryan was on the agenda for capturing the horse thief, but no action was taken; nor was there any explanation why no action was taken.

Then at the meeting on January 9, 1888, the county commissioners ordered Ryan's $250 bill stricken from the minutes and the matter held over until a later time.

On May 1, 1888, the prisoner made another attempt to escape, which was reported in the *Sundance Gazette* three days later. The article stated that Long (identified as Longabaugh) and Jim O'Conner escaped from their cell by crawling out of a 6" x 14" opening used to pass food to the prisoners.

When the jailer entered the hallway, the two men assaulted him. The jailer overpowered Long but O'Conner escaped, although he was soon recaptured. *The Gazette* also stated:

The Kid is the slippery cuss who gave Sheriff Ryan so much trouble, while bringing him to this place from Miles City.

On May 2, 1888, the county commission considered two separate $250 bills for the capture of Harry Longabaugh (Long): one was from Sheriff Ryan and the other from Miles City's Sheriff Irvine. Both requests for payment were disallowed by motion. The county commissioners must have realized the prisoner was an innocent cowboy and they were not going to pay the reward.

In November 1888 Sheriff Ryan opted not to run for reelection and the prosecutor who had William Long convicted was replaced by attorney H. A. Alden, who's first official act on taking office on January 22, 1889, was to forward a *petition of pardon* for the prisoner to the Wyoming governor.

On February 4, 1889, one day before his scheduled release, Long was granted a full pardon by Governor Moonlight. The pardon states he was under 21 years of age and his behavior has been good since confinement. Ironic, considering that according to court records he was 28 years old and had made two attempts to escape, assaulting the jailer in one of the attempts. [4]

During his incarceration, the newspapers referred to Long/ Longabaugh as "the Kid," "Kid Longabaugh," or "the Kid from Sundance." The name stuck. [5]

All subsequent newspaper articles, wanted circulars, Pinkerton files, magazines, and history books mistakenly state the Sundance Kid was Harry Longabaugh because of this miscarriage of justice in Sundance, Wyoming, in 1887. Because of this misidentification, Long's primary alias was Harry Longabaugh when he joined Butch Cassidy and his gang.

After his release, Long went to Deadwood, South Dakota, and later returned to Wyoming. On May 17, 1889, he was approximately thirty miles south of Sundance at Oil Creek with four men, one of whom was a wanted criminal named Bob Minor, alias Buck Hanby.

The men were in a dugout when Sheriff E. B. Armstrong and his deputy, James Swisher, charged in. When Minor went to get his gun, he was shot and killed.

Sundance must have threatened Deputy Swisher because Swisher filed a complaint against him on May 18, 1889, stating he had just cause to fear that he would be killed. No doubt Sundance was angry for being falsely imprisoned and viewed Swisher as part of the corrupt system that had framed him.

A criminal complaint was issued for Sundance, but the warrant was never served. He had left the area to avoid being arrested a second time. [6]

Sundance then went to the outlaw country around Cortez, Colorado, which he had become familiar with while passing through on cattle drives from Texas to Montana. At the time, Cortez was the outlaw capital of the Old West. It's where many of the outlaws first met and developed friendships that lasted many years.

The Cortez area was home to Robert Parker (Cassidy), Matt Warner, and the outlaw brothers Tom and Bill McCarty. Tom McCarty was married to Matt Warner's sister Teenie Christiansen and had a ranch near Cortez. [7]

Brothers Bill and Bert Madden lived in the area as well, as did Bert Charter.

After his time in jail, Sundance probably had a chip on his shoulder. He was drawn to the outlaw life and became acquainted with all these men. He would later rob trains and banks with some of them other than Butch. But the law was always looking for Harry Longabaugh as Sundance rather than Bill Long, family man of Fremont, Utah.

Neither local lawmen nor the Pinkerton's detective agents hired to track down outlaws had access to William Long's pictures from when he was a young man so they didn't realize until later on that Sundance and others were using aliases.

There was no fingerprint data base or DNA testing to confirm iden-tity. In William Long's case, lawmen never discovered who he really was, and that surely slowed down my own search. To this day, the true identities of some outlaws are still unknown.

NOTES
1. Elnora Frye, *Atlas of Wyoming Outlaws at the Territorial Penitentiary* (Laramie, WY: Elnora Frye, 1990, 273.
2. *Daily Yellowstone Journal,* June 7, 1887,
3. *Daily Yellowstone Journal, June 8, 18874. Daily Yellowstone Journal,* June 21, 1887.
4. Mary Garman, *Harry Longabaugh, the Sundance Kid: The Early Years, 1867-1889* (Sundance, WY: Crook County Museum, 1978), 5.
5. *The Sundance Gazette*, February 8, 1889.
6. Garman, *Harry Longabaugh, 5.*
7. Kelly, *Outlaw Trail,* 30. 31.

5
CHAPTER

New Life For Sundance

As a 15 year old in Levan, Utah Willard Christiansen got into an argument with Andrew Hendrickson over a girl. Christiansen went into a fit of rage and hit Hendrickson on the head with a large rock. The boy survived but suffered permanent brain damage.

After the fight, Christiansen immediately left town and went to the outlaw hideout Brown's Park. It was there he began his outlaw career by working for a cattle rancher and rustler named Jim Warner. Because of this association, Christiansen used the alias Matt Warner the rest of his life.

Matt Warner and Robert Parker/Butch Cassidy first met in a Telluride, Colorado, saloon in 1889. Warner owned a racehorse named Betty and while in town he entered Betty in a race. Unaware of Betty's speed Butch bet against the mare and lost his three saddle horses and gear to Warner. But instead of collecting, Warner told Butch to "keep his outfit and consider joining him in his racehorse venture."

Parker jumped into the partnership, and they traveled southwestern Colorado arranging races wherever they could and watched Betty bring in the money.

By this time, Warner's new brother-in-law, Tom McCarty, had established a ranch near Cortez. When Warner ran into McCarty at a Cortez saloon, he introduced him to Butch Cassidy.

Tom McCarty
(Courtesy of the Utah State Historical Society)

Apparently, all three hit it off well; they joined up and continued racing Betty. They won constantly, but just about as fast as they got it, the boys spent their winnings gambling and drinking.

Sundance arrived in Cortez after his release from jail. I personally think he went there to find Longabaugh at Harry's cousin's ranch. Longabaugh probably told Sundance about his cousin's ranch when they worked together in Miles City.

He didn't locate Longabaugh but he did find Warner, Cassidy, and McCarty. Sundance was good with horses and enjoyed saloons so the rowdy boys naturally became friends.

Warner, McCarty, and Parker raced Betty until they couldn't find anyone willing to go up against her. Perhaps out of simple boredom, or the desire for easy money, or just on a dare, they made plans to rob the San Miguel Valley Bank in Telluride.

Sundance was not involved but the trio invited Bert Madden to join their robbery crew.

The four men rode to Telluride a few days before the robbery. That sounds like Butch's M.O.: become familiar with the town, probe the defenses, case the bank, or maybe give everyone a chance to sober up and change their minds. I've heard many versions of the origin of the name Telluride; my favorite is an old timer there saying to a stranger, Because of all the crime and mayhem, the name came from "to hell you ride."

At noon on June 24, 1889, they went to the bank, ready to pull the heist. Madden remained outside on guard and holding the horses while the other three went inside the bank.

Warner had his gun under the cashier's nose before he knew what was happening. They demanded the money and got it. When the novice crew noticed the vault was open, Butch got the greenbacks and gold out of the vault and loaded them into the sacks too.

The robbers left with the then-staggering sum of $21,000. Split four ways that was $5,250, which in the 1800s was like hitting the lottery.

The four men rode leisurely away for a couple of blocks before spurring their horses into a full run and galloping away. No one chased them; it was a classic Butch Cassidy clean getaway.

Telluride's Sheriff Watson formed a posse that tracked the robbers' until the lost the trail at a creek. In his book *Last of the Bandit Riders*, Warner says when they reached the creek they packed their horses' hooves with gunnysacks and rode them across the rocks, making it look as if they disappeared.

For the next several days Sheriff Watson kept a close watch on everyone leaving Telluride and observed Bill Madden leaving town with a loaded packhorse. He followed Madden, and when he saw him hand the packhorse over to an unknown man, he arrested both of them. The sheriff found a letter on Madden from his brother Bert, asking him to pick up some supplies. The sheriff released Bill believing he would take the supplies to his brother Bert. But Bill Madden knew the Sheriff would follow him so, he led Watson on a wild goose chase rather than to Bert.

On July 1, 1889, *The Leadville Dailey and Evening Chronicle* reported:

Three of the Telluride bank robbers have been recognized, and it is now almost certain they will be captured. Their names are Tom McCarty, Matt Warner, and the younger brother of Billy Madden. Billy Madden is supposed to be implicated, as a letter from his brother to him has been captured by Sheriff Watson to prevent him from carrying out his promise. The fourth man is not known.

Of course the fourth man was Butch Cassidy. Once identified in the paper, McCarty, Warner, and Cassidy had to leave the area. They went to the familiar valley of Brown's Park and holed up in a cabin hideout that belonged to Warner's friend Charley Crouse.

As Warner tells it, "In a few days a ranch hand came racing to the cabin 'hell bent for leather' and told them that a posse was at Crouse's home after them."

Warner says there was only one safe place for them to go in the United States: Robbers Roost in Utah. They rode to the Robbers Roost in record time, traveling by night and hiding by day.

Warner describes Robbers Roost in his book, *Last of the Bandit Riders*:

Robbers Roost is the name of a Godforsaken section of country beginning about twenty miles east and southeast of Hanksville in the southeastern part of Utah covering the lower reaches of the San Rafael River to where it empties into the Colorado River. It is about seventy miles long, North and South, and fifty miles wide and is about the great-est natural rock fortress in the United States, and maybe the world. It is a regular jigsaw puzzle of deep, straight-walled canyons and deep, nar-row gorges with high mesas between. Some of the mesas are entirely surrounded by straight rock walls, sometimes a thousand feet high and more. We had a perfect natural rock fort.

Fortress Slot, Robbers Roost
(Courtesy of Kelly Taylor)

After you enter the narrow slot, you could keep the law off of you for days by just staying close to the other side of the opening, with guns at the ready, of course.

Robbers Roost Country
(Authors' Collection)

The Posse's Puzzle (Note Riders Below)
(Courtesy of Kelly Taylor)

They successfully hid out until Butch went to Green River, Utah, to get supplies, where he was recognized but he skedaddled out of there before they could catch him.

Surmising the bandits were hiding at Robbers Roost, Sheriff J. T. Farrer and two deputies went there determined to capture the fugitives.

Farrer and his deputies successfully followed the outlaw's trail into Robbers Roost but got lost on a side trail and ran out of drinking water. Knowing the sheriff and deputies would surely die if they continued on that trail, Warner left a note on a stick on the trail warning them.

Watching the posse from a distance, Warner fired his rifle and waved his hat to get their attention, motioning them to follow him. Warner led them to a natural spring and hid behind a rock as the posse drank and filled their canteens. He overheard the sheriff say; "Tom Farrer never goes back without his man."

Warner came out of his hiding place with his pistol in hand and demanded the men surrender. The lawmen gave up their guns. The three robbers discussed killing Farrer because of the sheriff's ungratefulness after they saved his life, but decided to humiliate him instead.

They took Farrer's saddle and hung his pants on a tree with a note that read, "Tom Farrer never goes back without his man, but he sometimes goes back without his pants." The robbers gave the three unarmed men directions to Hanksville and sent them on their way.

Sheriff Farrer had to ride his horse bareback in his underwear and with his shirt tail flapping in the breeze.

There are no saloons at Robbers Roost and the men soon got bored and wanted to leave for the excitement of town. The *Invincible Three"* as they called themselves headed for Lander, Wyoming. When they got near Lander Butch told the others it was too risky to go to town; the law was on the lookout for them and they might have been followed.

But Warner and McCarty were determined to go into Lander so Butch parted ways and told his compatriots he was going to the ranch of a friend named Brown. That was probably Cap Brown, the stolen horse expert. He and Butch drove the horses Butch stole in 1884 through Robbers Roost to Telluride to sell.

Butch's hunch proved correct. At the first Lander saloon they walked into, Warner and McCarty were having a drink when an old cowboy quietly told them, "A posse just rode into town inquiring for some strangers they been trailing. Maybe it ain't you, but I ain't going to stand around and see no stinking deputies grab good cowboys."

Warner said they nearly shook his hand off and were going to treat him to a drink when he said, "Don't stop for that. They will be here any minute."

As it turned out, the posse came in the front door while they were going out the back where their horses were tied. They mounted up and raced away with the posse shooting at them. Even with bloodhounds on their trail they managed to escape. [1]

In January 1889, five months before the Telluride bank job, Silas Morrell broke his back in a horrific accident at the Morrell Sawmill. Silas had been moving large logs with an employee named John Priestly the day of the accident. Priestly had dropped his end of one particularly heavy log, which caused Silas to lose control of his end. The log rolled loose and hit Silas, permanently damaging his back. After the accident, Luzernia grabbed her Browning 45-70 rifle, which is still in the family, and chased Priestly away. He never returned.

Silas became an invalid for the remainder of his short life, which profoundly impacted his family. Luzernia was left with the burden of financially supporting the family, caring for five children, the home-stead, working at the trading post, and perhaps worst of all, caring for an invalid husband who could not care for himself in the most basic of matters.

At an elevation of 7,300 feet, the winters in Fremont could be harsh. After careful thought and planning, the Morrell family believed if they moved to the warmer climate of the Mormon colonies of old Mexico, Silas's health would improve. So in March 1891, they traveled with two other families who were also moving to Mexico. Morrell's party included Luzernia's younger brother, Andrew Allred, who drove a wagon and Silas's father, William Morrell, a polygamist. In order to be admitted to the United States, Utah had to renounce the Mormon practice of polygamy. Rather than face persecution or possible prosecution, William decided to head south with Silas and his family. The Morrell's 14-year-old daughter Chloe drove the cattle on horseback.

They traveled eastward using the wagon road that is today's Highway 24. When they reached Caineville, they stopped to rest at the farm of Luzernia's sister, Nancy Allred Duncan.

Nancy later said, "How hard it was to see her sister leave with a sick husband while expecting a baby on such a long and harsh trip!"

When they reached Hanksville, they stopped at Charlie Gibbons's store, where Chloe met Gibbons for the first time. A year later she would go to work for him at the store and hotel.

After leaving Hanksville, they traveled south toward Hite's Ferry on the Colorado River at Dandy Crossing. It was spring, so water and forage could be found for the animals along this well traveled road.

They moved through Bluff, Blanding, and Monticello, Utah, to Dove Creek, Colorado. Once they reached Dove Creek, Luzernia went into labor. The men lowered the wagon's box onto the ground, where Ernest Morrell was born on the night of May 7, 1891. A very peculiar thing happened the next morning: when the men lifted the wagon box back onto the wagon's frame they discovered a bed of rattlesnakes right under where Luzernia had given birth.

Had the snakes bitten baby Ernest, he would have died within minutes. Had they bitten Luzernia, she would have died in hours and this story of the Sundance Kid would never have been told.

After a brief respite, they moved on and reached Cortez, Colorado, near the end of July. They stopped for a few days rest and then headed south to Farmington, New Mexico.

As they neared Farmington, they were completely disillusioned with the area and upset that they had made the long and harsh journey. The San Juan River was brown and muddy by the time it flowed through Farmington, whereas the Fremont River that flowed through their homestead in Utah was a beautiful, clear mountain stream.

Even worse than the water was Silas's health, which had progressively deteriorated on the journey. So they decided to return home to Fremont. They had come to the conclusion that Silas's condition was hopeless, and they wanted to take him home to die in as much comfort and peace as possible.

That September on their return journey, they were forced to make camp at a site just outside Cortez, for a while because they did not have enough money to buy fresh supplies. Thirteen year-old Chloe and 11-year-old Clara cleaned houses around town to earn money so the family could continue on.

The Morrell family history book includes a story Clara recounted about what happened in one of the homes where she worked during that time:

It was the days of the Wild West Cowboys coming to town. One time the cowboys came into town raising cane and shooting most of the night. The following morning I arrived at the home where I worked. The kitchen floor had been freshly scrubbed clean to hide the bloodstains, and two new graves were in the backyard. [2]

At that time, the Cortez area was home to cowboys and many outlaws so killings were common there, as they were in most of the wild towns of the Old West. Most of these cowboys did not have families living locally. Most came to town unattached, probably stopping for the recreation of saloons with gambling and brothels.

Sundance gravitated toward this kind of environment and lifestyle. He had a tendency to drink and didn't mind a good fight or a fancy lady.

One night that September for whatever reason—over a woman, over a horse, or over someone stepping on his foot and setting off his famously quick temper—Sundance was involved in a gunfight that left two men dead and him with a bullet hole in his right leg above the knee. His reputed skill as the fastest gunslinger no doubt saved his life that night.

Fortunately for Sundance it was dark outside, and he quickly left the saloon. He knew there were many travelers camped nearby so he went there to avoid any potential revenge seekers.

The Morrell layover at Cortez changed the destiny of William Long and the Morrell family forever. It was here that the Morrels met the Sundance Kid.

When Sundance came stumbling into the Morrell camp, he had lost a lot of blood. He was weak and needed help and a place to hide. Luzernia tended to his leg wound and allowed him to stay in their camp, giving him cover and possibly saving his life. Even though Luzernia was married and caring for her invalid husband Silas, there was a definite chemistry and attraction between her and Sundance.

When the Morrell family finally left Cortez to resume their trip home to Fremont, Sundance hid in their closed wagon. Over the next few weeks, he became well acquainted with the family. He saw a loving family doing what they could to ease the burden of the dying Silas. It's apparent that his affection for them was returned in spades. Sundance also sympathized and empathized with the Morrell family's financial plight.

Silas and Luzernia Morrell with Family
(Courtesy Viola Jackson Buchanan)

With possible lawmen or revenge seekers on his trail, it was too risky for Sundance to travel all the way to Fremont and risk the Morrell family getting caught in a gun fight. He stayed with them until he recovered enough strength to travel on his own. By the time he left, he and Luzernia were smitten with one another. He promised Luzernia that he would eventually go to Fremont to visit the family. He said his good-byes, saddled up, and rode off to Montana.

Around the exact same time Sundance was in Colorado and Utah, the real Harry Longabaugh was in Alberta, Canada, at High River, thirty five miles south of Calgary where he was enumerated on a census as a horse breaker on April 6, 1891.

That August he was charged with cruelty to animals, but the charge was dismissed a few months later.[3] In November he served as best man at Everett Johnson's wedding. [4]

In early 1892, Longabaugh and Frank Hamilton were partners in a saloon at the Grand Central Hotel in Calgary. The two men could not get along so the partnership soon dissolved. Later that year the hotel mysteriously burned down. [5] Longabaugh remained in Canada and worked with Everett Johnson, and as best as we can determine was a law-abiding citizen.

NOTES
1. Warner, *Last of the Bandits Riders…Revisited*, 8-59.
2. Eldon Morrell, Ancestors, and Descendants of William Wilson Morrell, 64.
3. Vicky Kelly, *Butch and the Kid*, (Alberta Canada: Glenbow Museum, Calgary, Canada) ,5.
4. *Big Hill Country*, 317–318.
5. Kelly, *Butch and the Kid*.

6
CHAPTER

A Bandit, and Then a Husband

Sundance left Utah and returned to Montana and worked as a cowboy for the rest of 1891 but was laid off in the winter in 1892. Later that year Sundance's friend Bill Madden from Cortez drifted to Montana and met up with him. They both were out of work and money.

Sundance and Madden surely had many conversations about the Telluride bank job Butch and the others pulled off and the $21,000 in loot they got. Eventually they decided to rob a train. They needed help tackling such a large job so they recruited Harry Bass.

At 3:30 a.m. on November 29, 1892, the three men waited for the Great Northern Railroad train to make its stop at Malta, Montana, where one of them boarded the train.

After the train cleared Malta, the robber climbed over the coal tender to the engineer's compartment. He put a gun to the engineer's head and ordered him to stop just up the track where the other two were waiting.

The conductor and the fireman went forward to the engineer's compartment to see why the train stopped. They were greeted by armed bandits who led the three trainmen to the express car. The conductor told the express messenger to open the door, which he did. The messenger was ordered to open the small safe, which held a few packages of little value, but they still took them. When they ordered the messenger to open the main safe, he told them he did not have the combination.

One of the bandits said, "I'm sorry for you young fellow, but it is a question of life or death for you. You either open the safe or die."

The messenger replied, "Well I am sorry, too, but its die I guess. I do not know the combination and cannot open the safe."

After a few moments, the bandits had second thoughts and rode away nearly empty handed. [1]

The Great Northern Railroad posted a $500 reward for each of the robbers, and the reward was matched by the state of Montana. [2] No easy money and a reward on your head. That had to sting a bit.

When the news of the "almost robbery" reached Glasgow, the Deputy Sheriff there and a posse went to Malta on December 1, following up on a tip the robbers were at Black's Saloon.

When the men saw the posse coming they grabbed their rifles and were ready for them when they entered the salon.

One of the bandits said, "Guess you deputies are after someone, ain't you? Well come right along, we'll make it interesting for you, and we'll take even bets or give you odds you don't take us. What do you say?"

The bandits had been drinking and would not go peacefully or without bloodshed. The posse wisely left the saloon. It was a stalemate; no money, no capture...at least not then.

Later in the day railroad detective Black arrived with deputies from several nearby towns and arrested two men who were boarding a train and two more men in town. The newspaper reported that one of the prisoners was named Ebaugh.

There was plenty of confusion as to who was involved in the attempted robbery; everyone had worn a bandana mask so Ebaugh was mistakenly released on December 8. [3]

Madden was one of the other men arrested and he was identified as Ebaugh's friend since they rode into town together. When Madden was asked, who Ebaugh was he answered "Harry Longabaugh." Madden would never tell them that Ebaugh was really his friend William Long. Madden learned from Sundance himself how he was framed and jailed as Harry Longabaugh so he just told them he was Harry Longabaugh. [4] It is doubtful that Madden ever knew the real Harry Longabaugh.

This is the first time that Sundance was identified as Harry Longabaugh since he left the Sundance Jail. Because Madden identified Long as Harry Longabaugh, Sundance would be identified as Longabaugh again when he robbed the same train again in 1901. Madden and Bass were tried, found guilty, and served time in the Montana State Prison. Technically at this point, Sundance was a fugitive with a price on his head so he did what wanted men do and left the state that was after him.

On September 6, 1893, brothers Tom and Bill McCarty, along with Bill's son Fred, robbed the bank of Delta, Colorado. As Tom was scooping up the cash, the teller shouted for help. Tom warned him to be quiet but the teller shouted again, and Tom shot and killed him.

The gunshot attracted attention and several men sounded the alarm. The McCartys immediately left the bank, mounted their horses, and started to leave town.

A storekeeper named Ray Simpson saw what was happening. He grabbed his rifle and intercepted the robbers as they emerged from an alley. Simpson killed Bill and Fred and shot Tom's horse but the animal made it to the relay horses and Tom escaped. He rode to southern Colorado and holed up in a one room cabin on the Dolores River near Cortez. Gene Grimes found him there badly shaken, grieving the loss of his brother and nephew. Tom recounted an interesting, coincidental story to Grimes that occurred prior to the robbery:

I stopped at a ranch that I had not been to in three or four years. Recently, the man had died, and the woman was trying to raise her kids. She had the best location in that part of the state, good grass and a nice stream of water that ran right through most of her range, and finally through her homestead.

It was a good outfit, but rundown a lot, when I pulled in. She was glad to see me, but there didn't seem to be much to eat in the place, and it looked poor. I couldn't figure it out until she told me her husband had been sick a long time, and it had cost them a lot of money. She said the banker had always wanted the ranch to build a summer home on, so he had loaned them the money and was coming out the next day to foreclose on the mortgage.

I had plenty of money with me—usually do—so I gave her the cash to pay off the mortgage. She didn't want to take it, but I told her it would be all right, wouldn't cost me anything.

The next day, I hid in the cedars and watched the banker ride in to collect his money. I couldn't hear what was said, but I could see he didn't like the deal a bit when he had to give her back the mortgage. Didn't rightly know why he had it with him. Just to gloat over her, I guess.

I made it a point to meet him down the trail apiece, and we had a little visit that cost him the profit on the deal. I didn't go back to the ranch, but she must have heard what happened, and I've wondered what she thought about it. [5]

McCarty, was probably referring to Luzernia Morrell when he told Grimes this story. It is a near perfect description of her and her family and homestead. Why he helped the family is unknown. Perhaps it was because of their friendship from the Trading Post days; perhaps because the loss of his brother and nephew weighed heavily on him, and he needed to rid himself of guilt; or perhaps it was just the plain old desire to help others in their time of need. I believe in the goodness in the heart of people and hope that was his reason.

By 1893 Sundance had kept his promise and worked his way back to visit Luzernia and her family. Sundance wanted to be near Luzernia so he got a job at the nearby Hogan Ranch, as a broncobuster for $35 a month. Today this ranch is called Paradise Ranch. The Hogan Ranch was a few miles north of the Morrell homestead on today's State Road 72.

In the summer, ranch hands rounded up wild horses from the nearby San Rafael Desert and drove them to the ranch where the broncobusters broke them. The horses were then sold to the United States Army at Fort Duchesne, Utah.

Hogan Ranch Today
(Courtesy of Brent Nickle)

While at Fort Duchesne dropping off horses Sundance met the quartermaster, Reuben Wilbur, [6] who mentioned that his stepson Bert Charter was working as a horse wrangler for ranches in the Little Snake River area on the Colorado/Wyoming border. Wilbur told Sundance Bert could get him a job there. So Sundance rode over to see Charter, and then returned to the Hogan Ranch.

Silas was still alive then and Sundance helped out as often as he could. It seems he wanted desperately to take care of the family he had emotionally adopted. I'm sure it had a lot to do with his early years as a runaway, having no family unit as a small, yet independent boy all alone.

Silas Morrell died September 26, 1893, from complications of his injuries suffered just four years earlier at the sawmill.

As a ranch hand, Sundance did not own a horse. On one occasion, he wanted to visit Luzernia, but all the available horses were in use by other cowboys, so he entered the corral with an unbroken wild horse while a few ranch hands looked on.

After a short few minutes on the horse, he had a cowboy unhook the corral gate and rode the partially broken horse down the road toward the Morrell's home. The horse was bucking and twisting as he went, and the cowboys laughed the whole time. But like a friend of mine says: "A man can't help who he loves and will be at her mercy for the rest of his life. Love isn't exchanged like currency; you have it and are stuck with it!"

Sundance claimed Luzernia cut his hair during his visits. Cowboys being cowboys, they ragged on him when he returned to the ranch: "*It took you six hours for a haircut? Was there something else she did for you?*"

Stone-faced Sundance would pay them no mind. His business was his business.

Over a short period, those haircuts ended up with Luzernia pregnant. One can assume they loved each other. Luzernia was Mormon and to avoid a church scandal, William Henry Long and Luzernia Allred Morrell were married on November 15, 1894.

Luzernia had a husband who loved her and her children and she loved him. He was a strong, strapping man who could protect and help support her and the children. At last Sundance had a family and on June 30, 1895, his first child, Florence Viola Long, was born.

Just two months after Sundance and Luzernia were married, Chloe Morrell (Sundance's oldest step daughter) married Jerry Jackson, who she met while working at Charlie Gibbons's store and hotel. They are my grandmother and grandfather.

The Morrell/Long homestead in Fremont was small by comparison to others in the area and at an elevation of 7,300 feet the growing season was short and most fruits and vegetables wouldn't grow there. The area is much more suited for raising cattle.

After several months, Sundance determined that he couldn't support his large family on such a small ranch. In order for him to fulfill every man's inherent responsibility to care for his family, he had to leave and find work elsewhere.

NOTES
1. *Daily Huronite,* December 2, 1892, *Daily Tribune,* December 3, 1892.
2. *Daily Huronite,* December 5, 1892.
3. *Daley Tribune,* December 3, 1892.
4. *Daley Tribune,* December 8, 1892.
5. Baker, *The Wild Bunch at Robbers Roost, 154–155.*
6. *Rawlins Republican,* March 02, 1893.

7
CHAPTER

Butch's Horse Business and Jail

After visiting his friend Cap Brown near Lander, Wyoming, Cassidy went back to Brown's Park, where he went to work for Herb and Elizabeth Bassett on their cattle ranch. Elizabeth was the backbone and boss as Herb wasn't even slightly interested in the doings of a working ranch. He would rather tend to the post office and his large library.

Cassidy took advantage of Herb's postmaster position by reading the newspapers and magazines that accumulated in the post office.

Herb believed everyone should be educated and allowed the ranch hands free rein of his library. Butch dived in and enjoyed many of Herb's books.

Cassidy became acquainted with Elza Lay, who worked for the Bassetts. Both men seemed to have the same calm and friendly disposition and became the best of friends in a short period of time. [1]

Butch courted the Bassett's daughters, Josie and Ann. The women both wanted Cassidy's attention and once physically fought over him. Cassidy didn't stay long in Brown's Park and one has to wonder if courting two sisters had anything to do with his abrupt departure.

Butch headed to the Wind River Basin and found work as a cowboy for the EA outfit, where he met Al Hainer. Obviously, they got along well because they soon quit the EA and formed a partnership to go into the horse trading business. [2] I use the term loosely.

They established a small ranch on Horse Creek in Fremont County, Wyoming. [3] According to author Charles Kelly "They always sold horses, never bought any." [4] Cassidy also became acquainted with Bub Meeks whose family owned a neighboring ranch. [5]

In the spring of 1890, Cassidy and Hainer sold all their horses then established another horse ranch on Blue Creek about ten miles northwest of the "Hole in the Wall" outlaw hideout. [6]

Cassidy left the ranch occasionally for a little cattle rustling on the side. He joined Matt Warner and Tom McCarty that summer of 1891. They circled the prairie country, picked up about fifty head of cattle, and set up camp by noon.

Butch spotted a group of riders coming for them with long range rifles; the bandits only had short range pistols. They quickly saddled their horses and galloped across the prairie while hotly pursued by rifle fire. In his book *Last of the Bandit Riders* Warner recalled, "They were so close, they shot between the horse's legs and knocked the fuzz of their ears."

Around sundown, they reached the Powder River and split up. Warner said he managed to escape by riding into the freezing river and I assume the others must've have escaped the same way.[7]

In August 1891, Cassidy and Hainer teamed up again for their horse-trading business. Before the month was up, Butch bought three horses from Joseph Billy Nutcher and secured a bill of sale for the purchase. Undoubtedly, he knew they were stolen. The following spring Butch and Hainer were arrested for stealing the three horses he had a receipt for. Butch had stolen horses in the past, but ironically he did not steal these horses.

Butch was released on bail and later acquitted of the charges. But while the first trial was still in progress, a second complaint was filed for the theft of a different horse than those named in the first complaint. Cassidy and Hainer were arrested again and released on bail for the new charge.

In late June 1894, Butch and Hainer arrived back in Lander for the second trial. Hainer was acquitted but Butch was convicted and sentenced as George Cassidy for two years at the Wyoming State Penitentiary at Laramie. Cassidy suspected Hainer double-crossed him in exchange for a not guilty verdict.

The obvious irony is that while Butch was guilty of many, many crimes, he was innocent of the one he was going to jail over.

George (Butch) Cassidy Penitentiary Mug Shot
(Internet Photo)

Butch was granted a pardon and released on January 19, 1896. He came out of prison determined to get even with the establishment that he believed had framed him. [8] Cassidy remained in Wyoming, visiting many of his old friends at different towns for a while.

He eventually went to Matt Warner's ranch in Brown's Park, where Cassidy, Bub Meeks, and Elza Lay made plans to commit another robbery.

The idea of planning another robbery annoyed Warner, who intended to quit the outlaw life and go straight. [9] Despite his stated good intentions, less than four months later Warner was arrested for killing Dick Staunton on the outskirts of Vernal, Utah. [10]

Cassidy needed money to hire a lawyer to defend Warner so he and his cohorts planned a robbery for that purpose. The three bandits went to work at a ranch outside of Montpelier, Idaho, for two weeks to become familiar with the town and establish possible escape routes.

On August 13, 1896, the three men rode into town leading a pack-horse. They tied the horses in front of the bank, leaving Meeks to tend them. Cassidy and Lay entered the bank with pistols drawn, ordering those inside *to raise* their hands, line up, and face the wall. Cassidy covered the customers while Lay went behind the counter and ordered the teller to give him the money.

The antagonistic teller told Lay there was no money. Without so much as a courteous warning or, I'll give you another chance; Lay whacked him across the forehead with his pistol and called him a "got damn liar."

After that the teller was quick to give Lay the bills from his drawer, which he threw into his money sack.

Lay then went to the open vault and took the bills he found there. On the way out, he grabbed gold coins that were on a counter and any other loose change he could find. He even took the teller's Winchester rifle.

Once outside, they mounted their horses and casually rode off until they reached the edge of town, where they spurred their horses and raced up the Montpelier Canyon. Reaching the fresh relay horses, they switched and rode hard toward Brown's Park.

A posse was organized and followed the robbers, but when they discovered the robbers' tired and sweating unsaddled horses milling about on the trail, the posse realized the bandits had relay horses and gave up the chase.

The amount of hard, cold cash taken was $16,500. [11] It was a mother lode of bucks for the time.

Unfortunately, the expensive lawyer did not prevent Warner from being convicted of murder.[10] A bank got robbed for nothing except, of course, the money.

By September 12, Cassidy was in Loa Utah where he checked into the Blackburn Hotel. According to a local newspaper report, Cassidy introduced himself as a cattle buyer and asked the proprietor for a copy of the Salt Lake City newspaper to see the latest news concerning the Montpelier Bank robbery. [12]

Blackburn Hotel and Livery Stable Where Butch Cassidy Stayed
(Courtesy of Brent Nickle)

While in the area Cassidy contacted his friend Sundance in nearby Fremont. They had not seen each other since meeting in Cortez six or seven years earlier. Cassidy told Sundance about the robbery, showed him the wad of money, and invited Sundance to join him for his next robbery. The sight of Cassidy's loot would have been very tempting for Sundance, especially since he could not support his family on the ranch income and knew he had to earn more money somehow.

Cassidy and Sundance had something in common. They had both been abused by the judicial system and served jail time for a crime they did not commit. But unlike Cassidy, Sundance did not intend to get even with the system; at least not yet.

Sundance decided to travel with Butch to Brown's Park, and from there he would go on to the Little Snake River and work with Bert Charter.

Sundance said goodbye to Luzernia and the children and left with Butch. On the way they stopped at the Behunin cabin in what is today the Capital Reef National Park. While there, Butch chiseled *"Butch Cassidy"* into the rear stone wall of the Behunin cabin, and Sundance chiseled "Sundance" on a large rock in the cave behind the cabin.

Behunin Cabin Capitol Reef, Utah
(Courtesy of Brent Nickle)

**Butch Cassidy Name on the Wall of Behunin Cabin
(Authors' Collection)**

**Sundance Name on a Cave Rock Behind the Behunin Cabin
(Courtesy of Brent Nickle)**

The Park Service has since removed Cassidy's inscription. Many of the locals are still a little upset over this, but the Sundance inscription still remains.

When they passed through Hanksville Cassidy left some of the Bank loot with Charlie Gibbons. [13]

NOTES
1. McClure, *The Bassett Women,* 57.
2. Lula Parker Betenson, *Butch Cassidy, My Brother* (New York: Penguin, 1976), 83.
3. Patterson, *Butch Cassidy, A Biography,* 46.
4. Kelly, *Outlaw Trail,* 53.
5. Patterson, *Butch Cassidy, A Biography,* 47.
6. Ibid., 50, 51.
7. Warner, *Last of the Bandit Riders...Revisited,* 83.
8. Patterson, *Butch Cassidy A Biography, 65-67.*
9. Warner, *Last Of The Bandit Riders...Revisited,* 113.
10. Ibid., 2.
11. Patterson, *Butch Cassidy, a Biography,* 88-92.
12. *Salt Lake Herald,* September 17, 1896.
13. Charles A Siringo, *A Cowboy Detective* (Charleston, SC: Forgotten Books, 2012), 347.

8
CHAPTER

Thanksgiving, Brown's Park, 1896

C assidy, Sundance, Elza Lay, and other outlaws were in Brown's Park in 1896 for Thanksgiving dinner where they served the local ranchers and their families the annual feast. The guests, of course, knew their servers were outlaws, but it didn't seem to bother them since everyone who came to their safe and quiet valley always behaved themselves. They all had a good time and good laughs that celebration day. Years later, Ann Bassett wrote of that dinner:

Poor Butch, he could perform such minor jobs as robbing banks and holding up Pay Trains without the flicker of an eyelash, but serving coffee at a grand party well, that was something else. The blood curdling job almost floored him; he became panicky and showed that his nerve was completely shot to bits. He became frustrated and embarrassed over the blunders he had made when some of the other hosts better informed told him it was not good form to pour coffee from a big black coffee pot and reach from left to right across a guest's plate to grab a cup right under their nose.

The boys went into a huddle in the kitchen and instructed Butch in the more formal art of filling coffee cups at the table. This just shows how etiquette can put fear into a brave man's heart. [1]

Ann said that there were at least thirty-five people there and one of the names she mentioned was Harry Rudenbaugh. This name would have been a reference to William Long's alias, Harry Longabaugh. [2]

Brown's (Hole) Park Colorado
(Internet)

When Cassidy and Elza Lay left Brown's Park, Ann Bassett joined them. They went south to Robbers Roost, where they spent part of the winter. Apparently, it was Ann's turn to be with Butch, or maybe her sister Josie didn't know about it. Butch did live a dangerous life. It's a wonder one of the Bassett girls didn't kill him.

**Butch Cassidy Campsite in the Robbers Roost
(Courtesy of Kelly Taylor)**

Elza Lay's wife, Maude, soon joined them at Robbers Roost. Maude later told her daughter Marvel that Etta Place was there that winter.[3] Maude was protecting Ann Bassett when she said that to her daughter. That sort of takes the mystery out of Etta Place's identity, at that point in time; Ann Bassett was the companion of Butch Cassidy. Later, she would be the companion of the Sundance Kid.

When Sundance went to work with Bert Charter, he used the alias Harry Alonzo, a reference to the two different people who were partly responsible for his imprisonment at the Sundance Jail: Harry Longabaugh stole Alonzo Craven's horse. The January 28, 1897, issue of *THE MINER* reported:

Charley Philbrick, Bert Charter, and Harry Alonzo passed through Dixon with their horses going to the mouth of Big Hole, where they will reside during the winter and look after the cattle interest of our stockmen, who are taking advantage of the mild winter to run cattle on the Powder Springs desert.

Sundance became acquainted with many outlaws in the Powder Springs area, including Harve Ray, Walt Punteney, George Currie, and Harvey Logan. He was also good friends with David Gillespie, who was a store clerk for Robert McIntosh in Slater, Colorado.

Sundance worked his trade breaking horses for the ranchers in the area. That spring or early summer, while working a horse, Sundance broke a rib and sustained a serious nasal injury. He returned home to Fremont to recuperate. There is no record that he ever broke horses for others again after that. The injury caused his nasal membranes and passages to become severely infected, resulting in a nasal inflammation called catarrh. This was confirmed by rancher Al Reader in a memo he wrote to the Pinkertons that stated, "Harry Alonzo has catarrh badly."

When forensic facial recognition expert Dr. McCullough examined the exhumed remains of Sundance in 2007, he discovered a healed fracture, a slight deformity of his skull at the bridge of the nose that was caused by an injury and would have resulted in a nasal infection. He also discovered that he had broken a rib.

While Sundance was recuperating in Fremont, Luzernia must have been cutting his hair again because she became pregnant with their second child Evinda. When he was healthy enough, Sundance traveled to the Little Snake River Valley and was there on June 27, and 28 to visit his friend David Gillespie as well as some friends at Al Reader's ranch. [4]

For the next three years, he worked and lived peacefully, becoming well acquainted with the people of Wayne County, from the farmers and ranchers in Rabbit Valley to the outlaws at Robbers Roost.

Here's an irony: on August 9, 1897, William Long was sworn in as a juror—almost exactly 10 years to the day he was convicted of Longabaugh's crime. Unfortunately there's no record of what the case was or the ultimate outcome. One can only wonder who showed up during deliberations: William Long or the Sundance Kid.

NOTES
1. McClure, *The Bassett Women*, 59.
2. The Ann Bassett Papers
3. Betenson, *Butch Cassidy, My Brother*, 121.
4. The David Gillespie Letter

9
CHAPTER

Castle Gate Robbery

E very time the train carrying the Pleasant Valley Coal Company payroll arrived in Castle Gate Utah from Salt Lake City, it would give a blast of its loud whistles letting let the miners know it was pay day.

Cassidy and Elza Lay had been in town a few days waiting for the train. It did not have an announced schedule precisely because of robbers looking to hold up the train en route. As usual they planned well but winged it when it came to what time the robbery would happen.

They had the best horses possible for the getaway. They raced up and back in town so the horses would become familiar with the potential commotion and the trains that came through. When some miners asked them why they were racing so much, they told them they were practicing for an upcoming race in Salt Lake City.

On April 21, 1897, Cassidy and Lay relieved the Coal Company of its payroll. When the train arrived, paymaster E.C. Carpenter went to the platform and received a satchel and three sacks of coins then headed back to the company's payroll office.

As Carpenter reached the office, Cassidy pressed a pistol against his head and quietly whispered in his ear, "I'll take that bag."

Carpenter was so surprised and fearful he just let Cassidy take the bag.

Holding the loot, Butch and Lay jumped onto their unsaddled horses and raced down the canyon toward Price. Apparently, three sacks of silver coins was one too many because they tossed one into a wagon they passed.

Not far out of Castle Gate they pulled up at a railroad section house where they had stashed their gear. They saddled their horses, cut open the satchel, and put the $8,000 in cash into canvas bags they had brought.

They met up with their accomplice Joe Walker. His job was to watch over their rendezvous point and cut the telegraph line to Price. E. C. Carpenter had to get a locomotive to take him to Price to sound the alarm. It's a little humorous that while Cassidy and Lay were transferring the loot, the train with Carpenter passed them on its way to Price.

The robbers had relay horses ready at certain points, as always, and they made a patented clean getaway to the Robbers Roost with a tidy sum $8000. [1]

I can't imagine why but the Pleasant Valley Coal Company immediately offered a reward of $2000 for the capture of the bandits. [2] The next day, the April 22, 1897, issue of the *Salt Lake Herald* reported Butch Cassidy was one of the robbers.

Safely in Robbers Roost, the three men set up camp with a luxury—tents. Their camp included three women: Millie Nelson, Maggie Blackburn from Loa, and cattle rustler Monte Butler and his wife, Ella. [3]

Cowboys Making Camp in the Robbers Roost
(Authors' Collection)

Many friends came and went from their campsite where they gambled, target practiced, and raced horses for amusement.

In one of the all night gambling sessions, Cassidy was cleaned out. He left the tent, and was soon back with a pocket full of gold and ready to gamble some more.

After a month or so the excitement of the Castle Gate robbery had quieted down and it was safe to leave the hideout. By that time the novelty of the camp had worn off and the weather was turning hotter, making Robbers Roost uncomfortable.

Cassidy headed home to visit his family. When he passed through Hanksville, Charley Gibbons joined him and together they continued on to Caineville where they stopped at my grandfather Jerry Jackson's Blacksmith Shop.

Except for one time in confidence to his wife Chloe, Jackson never admitted that he actually knew Cassidy. Jackson was probably the gang member or associate "Kid Jackson" that Charles Kelly mentions in his book Outlaw Trail, and if so this might explain his silence. Anyway grandpa distorted this particular encounter by saying that he went to the shop and found several of Cassidy's horses tied to the fence. He shoed the horses and tied them back where they were left. The next morning he found the horses gone and a twenty dollar gold piece on the anvil.

The next night Cassidy and Gibbons camped on Thousand Lake Mountain. It was about twenty miles from Fremont in a beautiful mountain meadow with a running creek.

While there, Cassidy carved *Butch Cassidy 1897* into a quaking Aspen tree. Some twenty feet from his carving is another tree on which Charlie Gibbons carved his name. Cassidy and Gibbons stopped and visited Sundance on their way to Loa. Sundance had just recently returned home to Fremont from the Little Snake River Valley.

Butch Cassidy 1897 Tree Carving
(Courtesy of Brent Nickle)

Gibbons had interests in Loa so Cassidy continued to Circleville on his own. After a short family visit, he traveled to Brown's Park where he hooked up with Lay. The two men wanted to celebrate and spend some of their Castle Gate robbery loot, but there were no saloons in Brown's Park. So along with some other outlaws, Cassidy and Lay hit all the towns along the Little Snake River. On July 29, 1897, they rode into Dixon, Wyoming, whooping, yelling, and shooting up the town. They rode on to Baggs, Wyoming, and finished off the celebration.[4] Cassidy then traveled to different parts of Wyoming and visited friends for the next several months.

Bud Meeks had been arrested in June 1897 at Fort Bridger, Wyoming, for the Montpelier Bank robbery. During his September trial he was identified as the accomplice holding the horses outside the bank. He was convicted and sentenced to thirty-two years in the Idaho State Penitentiary. [5]

For years newspapers had completely misrepresented Cassidy as a killer and attributed crimes to him he never committed. For example, the April 3, 1897, issue of the *San Francisco Call* erroneously stated that Cassidy was the leader of 500 outlaws who were armed to the teeth. It also reported there was least $20,000 in reward money offered for Cassidy, dead or alive.

With these self-serving and profanely false newspaper reports, Cassidy knew it was no longer safe to be in Utah, Wyoming, or Colorado.

In March 1898, the governors of Utah, Idaho, Colorado, and Wyoming met in secret to decide what to do about the outlaws. I think you know you've hit the big time when four governors gather to talk about you in particular. In April, Utah Governor Wells offered a reward of five hundred dollars for Butch Cassidy for the Pleasant Valley Coal Company robbery and other crimes. [6]

To make matters worse, on May 13, 1898, a posse led by Sheriff C. W. Allred of Carbon County, Utah, and Joe Bush killed Joe Walker, Cassidy's accomplice in the Castle Gate robbery.

Now that Bud Meeks was in prison and Joe Walker was dead, Cassidy and Lay had to face reality. They were wanted men for both the Montpelier and Castle Gate robberies. There was a big risk that they would be captured or turned in for the reward. Unlike other outlaws, Cassidy had the good sense to know when it was time to quit and leave, and that time was at hand. They opted to lay low for a while in Arizona and New Mexico and used different aliases to hide their identities.

Cassidy and Lay crossed the Colorado River at Lee's Ferry in Arizona, and then went on to Flagstaff where Cassidy visited friends. From there, they went to the Mormon settlements along the Little Colorado River. They drifted to southern Arizona and found work with the Erie Land and Cattle Company in Cochise County. [7] Here they befriended a cowboy named Perry Tucker, who got them work at the WS Ranch in Alma, New Mexico. At the WS, Cassidy and Lay used the aliases James Lowe and William McGinnis. [8]

NOTES
1. Baker, *The Wild Bunch at Robbers Roost,* 201-216.
2. Warner, *Last of The Bandit Riders*...Revisited 140.
3. Kelly, *The Outlaw Trail,* 152.
4. Ibid., 160.
5. Ibid., 162, 163.
6. Warner, *Last of The Bandit Riders*...Revisited 142.
7.. Nancy Coggeshall, *Hideout in the Gila, The New Mexican's Weekly Magazine,* 20-21.
8. William French, *Recollections of a Western Ranchman* (Silver City, NM: High Lonesome Books, 1997), 258.

10
CHAPTER

Belle Fourche Bank Job

Harvey Logan, George Currie, Harve Ray, Walt Punteney, and the serious whiskey drinking Tom O'Day planned to rob a bank in what they thought was a sleepy town; it was to be a "piece of cake" robbery.

O'Day was in town early on June 28, 1897, to scout the area and moseyed into a saloon to wait for the other four to arrive at the bank. O'Day in a saloon is like horses loose in stacks of hay; the hay will get eaten and the liquor will get drank.

Harvey Logan
(Internet Photo)

At 10:00 a.m., the four bandits rode up to the side entrance of the Butte County Bank in Belle Fourche, South Dakota, and tied up their horses. O'Day drunkenly left the saloon and walked over to the bank. He and Punteney remained outside as lookouts and got the horses ready to ride.

John Clay and Robert Robinson—the manager and assistant manager of the VVV Ranch where Harry Longabaugh stole the horse and gun in 1887— owned this bank. Inside the bank, the cashier and the accountant were preparing for the day's business. Six customers were in line waiting to transact business. Logan, Currie, and Ray entered the bank with guns drawn, shouting to everyone, "Hold up your hands!"

From across the street, store owner Alsom Giles saw the men inside the bank and walked over to investigate. When he opened the door and saw what was happening, he made a hasty retreat back to his store and sounded the alarm.

The three men heard the loud ruckus and grabbed $97 that a customer was about to deposit, and rushed out of the bank. They saddled up quickly, but Punteney and O'Day began shooting up and down the street to detract anyone one from coming toward them and frightened their own horses. Before the drunken O'Day had a chance to securely mount his horse, it bolted, and followed the other horses leaving O'Day on foot.

A posse chased them a few miles but soon gave up. The four bandits made a clean getaway. After some confusion as to O'Day's participation he was arrested and taken into custody.

A circular distributed by the Butte County Bank offered a reward of $625 for the capture of each of the four robbers identified as George Currie, Harve Ray and the Roberts Brothers. The circular included a description of the men. The four outlaws spent a few months in Wyoming at the Cook Stove Basin. George Currie left the group for parts unknown while Logan, Punteney, and Ray went to Red Lodge, Montana, intending to rob the bank there. I guess the big haul of $97 from the last bank job didn't go very far. But their luck wasn't much better in Red Lodge. They arrived in town September 18, 1897, to scout the area and Marshal Byron St. Clair recognized them. And they in turn recognized the marshal.

The outlaws informed St. Clair that they were going to rob the bank and suggested he go fishing. The marshal left briefly, informed the bank cashier of the pending robbery, and then returned to inform the men their presence was widely known, and they had better make tracks.

The bandits considered filling the marshal full of lead but voted it down and instead took his advice. [1]

The sheriff soon realized the men were wanted for the Belle Fourche robbery and there was a reward offered for their capture. A posse was formed to track down the bandits and collect the $1,875 in reward money. The leader of the posse was W. D. Smith, the same man who arrested William Long in 1887 near Miles City, Montana, as Harry Longabaugh.

Logan, Punteney, and Ray were traveling at a leisurely pace so the tenacious posse caught up to them before nightfall. Smith and his men decided to wait until the outlaws were settled in for the evening before confronting them.

As the bandits were making camp, they saw the posse closing in. Punteney jumped behind a rock ledge with his rifle to take cover. Ray grabbed his rifle and jumped on his horse, but before he could take any shots, his horse leaped over a narrow bluff, fell, and broke its neck.

After scrambling to his feet, Ray joined Punteney behind the rock ledge. Some shots were exchanged, but the robbers saw escape was hopeless so they surrendered. Logan, who was in the process of unsaddling his horse when the posse arrived, jumped on his horse and tried to escape. A posse member shot and killed his horse and wounded Logan, who then surrendered.[2]

They were taken to Billings, Montana, and put in jail. The bank authorities came on September 25, and had no trouble identifying the three men as the bank robbers.[3] The robbers were then taken to the Lawrence County jail in Deadwood, South Dakota, to await trial.

Logan and Ray claimed they were brothers Tom and Frank Jones. However, Punteney had already confessed his real name. [4]

Remember that outlaws would use the aliases of other outlaws to confuse law enforcement. This is exactly what Ray did. Ray's attorney asked David Gillespie, a friend of Harry Alonzo (Sundance), to come to Deadwood and give him an alibi.

Ray knew Alonzo (Sundance) and Gillespie were friends, so when he sent his message, it stated that he (Ray) was Harry Alonzo. Ray believed once Gillespie was in Deadwood, he would commit perjury and identify him as Harry Alonzo (Sundance), thereby giving him an alibi and giving him a get out of jail free card.

Gillespie knew that Alonzo (Sundance) had been in the Little Snake River Valley on June 27 and June 28, and assumed he had left in early August to join the outlaws and was mistakenly captured along with the robbers.[5] But Sundance did not join the outlaws when he left the area. He went home to Fremont and was there by the middle of July.

Gillespie could not go to Deadwood, but other friends of Alonzo/ Sundance did go, believing Ray was Alonzo. The October 30 issue of the *Rawlins Journal* reported:

Harry Alonzo, who formerly worked for Reader & Co. cattle outfit at Snake River, and who had joined the Powder Springs gang of thieves sometime last winter, was arrested about a month ago in South Dakota on charges of robbing the Belle Fourche Bank. Alonzo wrote down to some friends who had previously known him to come up and identify him. J. Galloway and E. Lahey of Baggs went to Pierre, S.D., but the officers who had charge of Alonzo refused to allow him to be seen, claiming he had been identified by the bank employees as one of the bank robbers and that the reward of $1,800 had been paid for his arrest. As a matter of fact, Alonzo (Sundance) was on the Snake River at the date of the bank robbery, working for Reader & Co.

It doesn't make sense that Galloway and Lahey would be denied access to the prisoner. They did see the prisoner and knew he was not Harry Alonzo and they were not going to be stool pigeons or commit perjury. They simply told the newspaper they were not allowed to see the prisoner.

Believing they would be convicted and sentenced to prison, the inmates overpowered the jailer and escaped the Deadwood jail on October 31, 1897.

Harvey Logan's brother Lonnie assisted in the escape by providing the horses for Harvey and Ray, but not for Punteney and O'Day so those two were soon captured. Logan and Ray, however, made a successful escape.

There was a wanted circular distributed with their description and a $150 reward for their capture. The circular gave their names as brothers Frank and Tom Jones. The description of Tom Jones matches Harvey Logan. The height for Ray, aka Frank Jones, is given as 5'10 ½." This is more proof that this was not Harry Alonzo (Sundance) whose height was 5'9." [6]

The following year an article appeared in the February 27, 1898, issue of the *Deseret News*:

Harve Ray and others that escaped from the Belle Fourche bank robbery, were joined by a party of Powder Springs' thieves and were driving a large herd of stolen cattle to Hole in the Wall.

Bandits in the Rearview Mirror
(Courtesy of Christine Karr)

NOTES
1. *Anaconda Standard,* July 21, 1901.
2. *Billings Gazette,* September 24, 1897.
3. *Nebraska State Journal,* October 2, 1897.
4. *Eau Claire Leader,* September 28, 1897.
5. The David Gillespie letters.
6. Bob Lee interview, Hadsell Papers from the Meschter Collection, Casper Chapter.

11
CHAPTER

The Wilcox Train Robbery

T he gang did not commit any robberies during the entire year of 1898 except for a little cattle rustling. During the summer of 1899, George Currie, Harvey Logan, and Harve Ray reunited and decided to rob a Union Pacific train.

It had been raining for some time near Wilcox, a lonely station on the Union Pacific train route about thirteen miles southeast of Medicine Bow, Wyoming.

It was still raining heavily at two in the morning of June 2, 1899, when locomotive engineer, William R. "Grindstone" Jones, saw the flashing lanterns—one red, one white—down the tracks. It was a warning signal so he brought the Overland Flyer to an abrupt stop about a mile past the old Wilcox station.

Immediately, three masked and armed men appeared on both sides of the engine. Two of them boarded the compartment, ordering Jones and his fireman, John Walsh, to get out. They then led the two trainmen along the track back to the first mail coach. Burt Bruce, the clerk in charge, extinguished the lights and locked the doors.

The robbers hammered on the door and fired two rifle shots into the car as a warning. They ordered Bruce to unlock the doors, which he did, and joined the other two hostages. The robbers only wanted what was in the express car but had to check for weapons and the number of people in the mail car.

As the outlaws marched the crew to the express coach, they saw the headlight of an approaching train that was only a few minutes away. The train crew explained it was a special personnel train with soldiers on board.

Nervous, the bandits ordered the two passenger cars uncoupled from the rest of the train. The crew was taken back to the engine, where the robbers ordered the engineer to move the train farther up the track over a bridge and away from the passenger cars.

It took a few moments for the train to move after the brakes were released. One of the robbers thought the engineer was stalling and pistol whipped him.

One of the other robbers, apparently the leader of the bunch, admonished the man, saying, "Hold on there. We don't want any killing about this!"

After moving the train, the robbers blew up a portion of the bridge to stop the troop train. The explosion didn't destroy the bridge, but the damage was sufficient to prevent traffic from crossing it.

The engine and cars were then run to the top of a hill, where one bandit held the crew hostage at rifle point while the other two hammered on the locked express car door.

The express messenger, Charles Woodcock, told the robbers that he would shoot anyone who entered. The outlaws used dynamite and blew a hole in the side of the car, which knocked Woodcock unconscious. They tried to revive him to get the safe combination, but he was too shaken to remember it and probably did not know it anyway.

Woodcock had to be helped from the car. Using dynamite again, they blew the top of the safe off, which also destroyed the car. They took the paper money, which was damaged by the explosion.

The robbers fled the scene, going north to the "Hole-in-the-Wall." Posses from Rawlins, Laramie, and Casper banded together north of Casper to follow the robbers.

The Wilcox Express Car
(Internet Photo)

Over one hundred miles north of the robbery scene, on June 3, the posse camped for the night at Castle Creek, with the bandits camped only about four miles away.

Early the next morning, Sheriff Josiah Hazen went out scouting and saw the robbers walking up the creek to get their horses. When the outlaws saw Hazen, they moved down the creek and hid, but Hazen found their trail and followed it. When he confronted the men, they shot him and escaped. Sheriff Hazen was taken to Casper and then to Douglas, where he died on June 7. [1]

Despite the lawman's murder, local ranchers harbored the robbers and obtained horses for them. The outlaws found out that a militia was stationed at the eastern entrance of the Hole-in-the-Wall, so they swung around and headed for Utah. [2]

The bandits split up and went in different directions to make it more difficult to be followed, and they all vanished in the countryside. (After this robbery George "Flat Nose" Currie went to Castle Dale, Utah, and rustled cattle. The following year while rustling cattle Sheriff Jess Tyler killed him on April 17, 1900.

Harvey "Kid Curry" Logan avenged the death of his mentor by murdering Sheriff Tyler and his deputy Sam Jenkins in cold blood on May 17, 1900.)

The Pacific Express Company and the Union Pacific Railroad offered a $2,000 reward for each bandit, dead or alive. Killing Sheriff Hazen had put a larger than usual bounty on the robbers' heads so they were constantly looking over their shoulders. And because the money was slightly burnt and had one corner missing, the Pinkertons could easily trace it.

On January 15, 1900, former Pinkerton detective Tom Horn wrote a letter to the railroad's division superintendent in Cheyenne, Wyoming, informing him that he had gone to rancher Bill Speck's house on January 2 and stayed there for four days.

On the fourth day, Horn told Speck he wanted information about the Wilcox robbery and would kill him if he didn't get it. Speck began to cry and told Horn what he knew: the robbers were George Currie, Harve Ray, and a man he did not know, who turned out to be Harvey Logan. [3]

Lonnie Logan had furnished the horses for his brother and Ray when they escaped the Deadwood jail two years earlier.

Still owing Lonnie for the horse, Ray paid him with the damaged Wilcox money, mailed from near Galveston, Texas. [4] That was the last anyone heard of Ray. He disappeared and was never brought to justice.

The Pinkertons traced the damaged money to Lonnie in Landusky Montana. When Lonnie got wind of the Pinkertons' discovery, he traveled to his aunt's house in Dodson, Missouri. The Pinkertons eventually learned more of the damaged money had been spent in Dodson and closed in on Lonny. He was shot and killed on February 28, 1900, while attempting to escape the dogged Pinkerton detectives.[5]

Bob Lee received considerable part of the stolen money from either Harvey or Lonnie, but he was never actually involved in the robbery. Ironically, though, Lee was the only person ever tried and convicted for the Wilcox robbery and served seven years in the Wyoming State Prison. [6]

Soon after the Wilcox robbery, the Union Pacific Railroad hired the infamous Pinkerton Detective Agency. In addition to their base fee, the Pinkertons were paid additional money for each outlaw captured or killed.

The Pinkertons assigned Charles Siringo and W.O. Sayles to the Wilcox case. The detectives discovered that during his escape, Harvey Logan went through Thompson, Utah, where he spent some of the damaged loot. In Hanksville, Utah, he spent more at Charlie Gibbons' store. [7] Logan then went south to the WS Ranch in Alma, New Mexico, where Cassidy was still working but without his friend Lay, who had recently quit.

Cassidy wanted to retire from the outlaw life and go straight but Lay didn't and the years of friendship ended when Lay left the ranch and signed on with outlaws Sam Ketchum and Will Carver to rob a train.

On the night of July 11, 1899 Lay, Ketchum, and Carver held up a Colorado Southern train at Folsom, New Mexico. The safe was blown with dynamite and at least $50,000 was taken. A posse picked up trail the next day and followed it.

On July 16, the robbers were camped for supper when the posse found them and a gunfight commenced. Lay was on his way to the creek for some water when he was shot in the back and shoulder. Ketchum was wounded and so were two posses members named Frank Smith and Henry Love. Smith eventually recovered but Love died.

In the exchange Lay shot Sheriff Edward Farr in the chest, killing him. Their leader dead, the posse retreated, allowing the robbers to escape.

Wounded and needing rest, the robbers went to an empty cabin owned by Ed McBride. As soon as Lay and Carver were able to travel they left, but Ketchum was too weak so he was left behind.

The next day, McBride and his family returned to their cabin and found Ketchum. They bandaged his wound and turned him in to authorities. Ketchum died of blood poisoning on July 24.

A month later a rancher named John Lusk notified Eddy County Sheriff M. C. Stewart about two suspicious men staying at his cabin. The sheriff and his posse rode out to Lusk's cabin to investigate.

Lay was alone eating breakfast when he heard the posse arrive. Lay rushed out and shot Deputy Rufus Thomas in the shoulder and wounded Lusk in the wrist. The Sheriff fired a shot that grazed Lay's head, stunning him. Lay was quickly disarmed, tied to a horse, and taken to town.

Lay was charged with the murder of Sheriff Farr. During the trial, Lay identified his accomplices as the dead Sam Ketchum and G.W. Franks, Will Carver's alias. [8] No way would he be a stool pigeon and give Carver up.

On October 10, 1899, Lay was convicted for the murder of Sheriff Farr and sentenced to life in the New Mexico Territorial Penitentiary. He was released after serving less than seven years. [9] I guess life means 7 years in New Mexico.

Matt Warner claimed he and Lay bribed the warden and the governor with a con story about a nonexistent asphaltum mine that Lay signed over to them for an early release. [10]

Elza Lay
(Internet Photo)

When Logan arrived at the WS Ranch, using the alias McGonigal, the peaceful cowboy life that Cassidy had enjoyed for the previous couple of years ended. Logan bought some horses from a ranch hand using burnt loot money, which the Pinkertons eventually traced back to the WS Ranch. In August 1899, the Denver Pinkerton office sent Agent Frank Murray to investigate. He showed ranch manager William French a picture of several people, one of which French knew as Jim Lowe, a trail boss. Murray told French that the man he knew as Jim Lowe was really Butch Cassidy, the brains behind and leader of the most organized gang in a generation. He also informed French that the Pinkertons were willing to pay a reward for his capture.

French asked Murray if he intended to arrest Cassidy and he said no. He told French the gang was undoubtedly getting inside information on express shipments. In my opinion Murray himself was the one that was telling the gang what trains had shipments of money or gold. Returning to Denver, Murray never reported to his superiors that Cassidy was in Alma.

French told Cassidy about Murray's visit, which Cassidy already seemed to know and said he was not worried at all and said he had bought Murray a drink at the local saloon before the detective left for Denver. Even though Cassidy told French he had no intention of immediately leaving, his instinct told him it was time to move on. [11]

Cassidy's good friends Elza Lay, Bud Meeks, and Matt Warner were in prison. Joe Walker, Sam Ketchum, Bill, and Lew McCarty were dead. Cassidy was a wanted man with a reward on his head.

Cassidy, as always, had a plan. He went to Salt Lake City where he met with Judge Orlando Powers in an attempt to get Utah Governor Wells to grant him a pardon. Cassidy told Powers he wanted to quit the outlaw life before he became the next victim of the relentless Pinkertons or a bounty hunter. Even though Powers was sympathetic, he told Cassidy that a judicial pardon was impossible. He suggested

Cassidy leave the country and make a new start someplace where he was unknown.

Cassidy thanked him for the advice and said: "You'll never know what it means to be forever on the dodge."

Unaccustomed to giving up, Cassidy persuaded his friend Sheriff Parley Christiansen to arrange a meeting with the Utah Governor.

The sheriff and Butch pleaded his case to Governor Wells but again Butch's request for a pardon was denied. Sheriff Christiansen believed that the governor's refusal was responsible for the crimes that Cassidy committed after that time.

Judge Powers then had an idea he thought would make all parties happy. He contacted the Union Pacific Railroad and suggested they pay Cassidy a salary to be a guard on their trains. With Cassidy on the train as a guard Powers believed other outlaws would not rob the trains. Cassidy and the railroad liked the idea so they agreed to meet and finalize the deal.

Cassidy's attorney, Douglas Preston, was assigned to bring the railroad representatives to Lost Soldier Pass, Wyoming, for the meeting. But a snowstorm delayed the group and they missed the scheduled appointment.

When the attorney and the railroad men finally arrived, Cassidy was gone but he had left them a note: "Damn you Preston, you have double crossed me. I waited all day, but you didn't show up. Tell the UP to go to hell and you can go with them."

Wanting to live free and in peace, Cassidy tried everything he could to get a pardon but failed. He could no longer live in obscurity as a cowboy in the United States. He had tried that in New Mexico, but it wasn't to be.

At that time, many American cowboys were going to Argentina and finding work in the cattle business. Cassidy decided to follow suit and start a new life as a cattle rancher and hopefully live in peace and obscurity. But he needed some money to start a new life, and he knew how to get it. Toss a coin, bank or train!

Meanwhile, Judge Powers had another idea that he discussed with Governor Wells, who got on board with it.

Powers contacted Matt Warner, out of prison since January 1900, and paid him $175 in travel expenses to find Cassidy. His job was to explain why the group missed the Lost Soldier Pass appointment and present him the railroad's offer.

Matt Warner
(Internet Photo)

Warner left Salt Lake City the last week of August 1900 by train, bound for Rock Springs, Wyoming. When the train reached Bridger Station, the conductor handed Warner a telegram.

"All agreements off. Cassidy just held up the train at Tipton." [12]

NOTES

1. *Rawlins Republican,* June 17, 1899.
2. *Anaconda Standard,* July 21, 1901.
3. Chip Carlson, *Tom Horn Blood on the Moon* (Glendo, WY: High Plains Press, 2001), 94.
4. Bob Lee interview, Hadsell Papers, Meschter Collection, Casper College.
5. Kelly, *Outlaw Trail,* 260.
6. Bob Lee interview, Hadsell Papers, Meschter Collection, Casper College.
7. Siringo, *Cowboy Detective,* 312.
8. Jeffrey Burton, *Deadliest Outlaws,* (Dallas Texas: University of North Texas, 2012)165-189.
9. Kelly, *Outlaw Trail,* 251–255.
10. Warner, *Last of the Bandit Rider. .Revisited,* 131-132.
11. French, *Recollections of a Western Ranchman, 258–274.*
12. Kelly, *Outlaw Trail,* 266–272.

12
CHAPTER

The Tipton and Winnemucca Jobs

Sundance had been living quietly at home in Fremont as a devoted family man since August 1897. In January 1900, he visited Mormon faith healer, Dr. Elias Blackburn, who treated a cancer that had developed on Sundance's lip. [1]

Blackburn asked, "Do you believe?"

Sundance replied, "Hell, yes, Elias, I believe, or I wouldn't have come here." [2]

The cancer cleared up, but left a permanent scar.

Sundance experienced a huge change in attitude toward his family and life in Fremont that January. The nasal injury from three years earlier had worsened and developed into an infection, which could have been a factor in his behavior.

Viola and Evinda Long
(Courtesy of Gaylen Robison)

In June 1900, Sundance went to Montana to visit old friends. A local named J.D.B. Grieg recognized him and wrote a letter to Pinkerton informing them that Sundance was in Culbertson with two cowboys that he formally worked with at the N Bar N Cattle Company.

Grieg also acknowledged that he was implicated in the Malta train robbery several years prior. I'm sure Sundance didn't know of this letter. Otherwise, he may have shot Grieg for his treachery.

When Sundance returned to Utah it was not home to Fremont. According to the 1900 census, Sundance was no longer listed as living with Luzernia, who was designated head of household on the census.

Even though Sundance wasn't there, the census taker still needed to record birthplace of the father of Viola and Evinda. Since he had never told her, Luzernia guessed. All she really knew was that when he wasn't home in Fremont, he was working for the ranchers in Wyoming, so she assumed that this was where he was born and gave that as his birthplace.

Sundance himself was enumerated on the 1900 census between July 10 and July 20 at a logging camp near Vernal Utah, at the Clear Creek precinct with his friend and future stepson-in-law Charles Anderson. However, Sundance was not actually there. By this time, he had left to join up with Cassidy. So it was up to Anderson to answer the census taker's questions as best he knew and making up the rest.

Anderson gave Sundance's occupation as a log cutter and gave his age as thirty-six. However, his actual age was thirty-nine. Sundance had once told Anderson about the time he spent in Montana during the 1880s and 1890s and because of his recent visit there Anderson assumed he was born in Montana and gave that as his birthplace to the census taker. The census record also gives Sundance's father's birthplace as Missouri, but he was born in Ohio. The record gives his mother's birthplace as Kentucky, but she was born in England.

In early July 1900, Sundance was with Butch Cassidy at the Brown's Palace Hotel in Denver, Colorado, where they met Jack Ryan, the gang's go-between with an insider, probably Pinkerton detective Frank Murray that knew which trains had shipments of money for a share of the loot.

While in Denver, Sundance's nasal catarrh infection flared up again, and he had some nasal tumors removed at a local hospital.

In late July or early August, Cassidy, Sundance, and Harvey Logan met in Ogden, Utah, at Jack Egan's saloon where they agreed to split up the gang, commit two separate robberies, and then meet back at Brown's Park.

They decided one target would be a Union Pacific train and the other the First National Bank in Winnemucca, Nevada.

Logan wanted Sundance with him for the train robbery. The Pinkerton files state: *"Sundance at first agreed to join Logan for the train robbery but decided to join Cassidy for the bank robbery instead. Sundance sent word to Logan by Jim Ferguson he could not keep his appointment."*

Sundance probably decided that it was safer with Butch since the past several robberies for Logan didn't go too well, including the murder of Sheriff Farr.

Logan needed another man to replace Sundance and Ferguson suggested William Cruzan.

Around 8:30 p.m. on August 29, 1900, Harvey Logan, Ben Kilpatrick, William Cruzan, and Perry "the dynamiter" robbed the Union Pacific No. 3.

While the train was stopped at Tipton, Wyoming, one of the outlaws quietly slipped aboard. Soon after the train left, the masked bandit climbed over the coal tender to the engineer's compartment with a gun in each hand.

He pointed one at the engineer's head and the other one at the head of the fireman and ordered the engineer to stop the train at a campfire along the track, where the other three robbers were waiting.

When the conductor got off the train to see why it had stopped, the bandits ordered him forward to the locomotive.

The coach cars were uncoupled, then the express and mail cars were moved farther down the track and stopped. The express messenger, Woodcock, at first refused to unlock the car door but the conductor convinced him to comply. Woodcock had reason to be hesitant as he had been the express messenger at the Wilcox robbery over a year earlier where he was knocked unconscious by the dynamite explosion.

It took three separate dynamite charges to blow the safe open, which coincidently, again destroyed the express car. Taking the money and some jewelry, the robbers mounted their horses and rode off into the darkness and to Brown's Park.

The railroad and the express companies said "little was taken," but Woodcock let it slip to the press that the actual loss was $55,000. The meeting in Denver with the corrupt insider had paid off handsomely.

A posse trailed them for over a week but the gang made a clean getaway. Union Pacific general manager E. Dickenson offered a reward of $1,000 for each of the four robbers, dead or alive. [3]

The Pinkertons assigned their ace detective Charles Siringo to the case as an undercover agent. Using the alias Leroy Davis, Siringo was able to gain the confidence of a few gang members and traveled with different members as a trusted friend.

Siringo was traveling with Bert Charter when the outlaw got a tip while they were passing through Dixon, Wyoming, that the Pinkertons had a cowboy detective named Charlie Siringo working with the Wild

Bunch to get their secrets. Charter suspected that his traveling friend Leroy Davis was Siringo, but the detective convinced Charter that he was not the Pinkerton detective. Siringo was confident he was betrayed by one of the assistant superintendents from the Denver office, either Goddil or Frank Murray. [4]

Charles Siringo In Hanksville, Utah
(Internet Photo)

In early September 1900 Butch, Sundance, and Will Carver set up camp fourteen miles east of Winnemucca, Nevada. The three men rode into town each day to become familiar with its layout.

They became acquainted with some of the locals who told them about different routes and shortcuts. The outlaws also picked up information about the First National Bank and its personnel. The outlaws decided to rob the bank on September 19.

Winnemucca, Nevada Bank Today
(Authors' Collection)

The Pinkerton files have an interesting account of the robbery from a person identified as Informant #85:

They met a man they knew, and he told them about the Winnemucca Bank being dead easy. This man worked for a time for Nixon (Senator Nixon) and I think he was in a position to know something about the bank affairs so, they watched things while staying on the river at the ranch close to town. The morning they came into town to rob the bank they came across a field and cut the fence at a place this man (referred to above) told them about so they could use it and no one else could get through that way. Bill Carver had a couple of blankets rolled up and tied with a couple of straps. He had on "hobnailed shoes" and looked like a tramp. Inside the roll of blankets he had a sawed-off 30-40 carbine. Just after cutting the fence they separated.

Jim Lowe [Cassidy] and Sundance came in town first. Bill Carver stopped on the way to kill a skunk but got the worst of the battle. After killing the skunk he came into town and tied up his horse and stood near the bank (I think at the public watering place).

Anyway he was there waiting for a tip that the coast was clear. During the time that Carver was there waiting, an old couple stopped and talked to him and "roasted" the town for being so slow.

"They said it should be dead and buried." Bill said he told them that if they waited around for a while things would be pretty lively.

The old man said, "Say, stranger, what's going to happen, earth-quake, or something?"

Bill replied that it would be worse than that. Just then the coast was clear, and the boys strolled down to the bank. Sundance and Jim Lowe went in first. Bill came in last with the roll of blankets and sat them on end between his knees and began to fumble in his pockets while the other two covered the outfit. Then Bill comes up with his sawed-off and covers them also. Jim climbed over the railing and gathered up the dough.

As they came out of the bank this old party, before mentioned, sees them and yells, "Robbers" so Sundance drops a couple (shots) under the old man's feet. The old man and the old lady started to run up the street with the old lady yelling for them "not to shoot pa, as he won't harm you-uns."

Bill Carver said the old man's coattails were sticking out straight behind. The boys said the clerks in the bank kept sniffing, and Bill said he could hardly stand it himself. This was on the account of his battle with the skunk.

They dropped one sack of money on the street, and Jim Lowe turned back to get it. When the people saw him coming, they all broke for cover as they thought he was coming back to kill them, so they got out of the way. The boys rode all that day and cached their money and changed their cloths and separated, each going his direction to meet later.

Carver's cloths stunk like hell.

The local *Silver Slate* newspaper published this article on the day of the robbery:

Around noon the three robbers entered the Winnemucca National Bank and two of them, with guns drawn said, "Gentlemen, throw up your hands, be quick about it, and don't make any noise."

The third robber burst into the cashier's office and with rifle drawn ordered the cashier and a customer to the front room of the bank with the others. One robber ordered the cashier to open the safe to the vault while the other two covered the rest of the people. Three sacks of gold were taken plus the gold that was in the teller's money drawer, leaving silver and paper money. They took the employees and customers out the back door, and then the robbers jumped over the fence and ran down an alley to where their horses were tied.

They mounted and were leaving town when Sundance dropped a bag of gold. He stopped, dismounted, picked it up, handed it to a pal, mounted up, and they rode away.

The railroad tracks ran parallel to the road the bandits used in their escape, so a posse left Winnemucca by train. They fired a few shots at the bandits and then returned to Winnemucca. [5] Even though there were several mounted posses in pursuit, the robbers made a clean getaway, going north then east to the Idaho border.

It was a typically well-planned Butch Cassidy style robbery with no one killed and fresh relay horses ready at designated points along the escape route.

The Winnemucca robbers joined up with the Tipton robbers by early October and were safely nestled in their Brown's Park hideout. The American Bankers Association offered a $2,000 reward for each one of the bandits, dead or alive. But it was never collected.

The Pinkerton investigation discovered that one of the robbers was the same man identified as Harry Longabaugh while incarcerated in the Sundance, Wyoming jail in 1887. They discovered that Longabaugh was originally from Pennsylvania, and he had relatives still living there. They discovered that Longabaugh visited his brother Elwood in San Francisco in 1900. But the Pinkertons never discovered the man in the Sundance jail was in fact William Long, not Longabaugh. A reward was offered for Harry Longabaugh although ole' Harry was completely innocent of the crime.

After the Winnemucca bank robbery, Longabaugh found out he was wanted for bank robbery so he used an alias and disappeared for good. Longabaugh got a karmic taste of his own medicine being wanted for something he did not do.

Because William Long was mistakenly identified as Harry Longabaugh in the Pinkerton records, everything published since then has mistakenly identified the Sundance Kid as Harry Longabaugh. (I find that very amusing.)

NOTES
1. The Blackburn Journal, Utah State Historical Society.
2. Earl Jackson Interview by Jerry Nickle.
3. *Rawlins Republican,* September 1, 1900.
4. Siringo, *Cowboy Detective,* 366.
5. Kelly; *Outlaw Trail,* 279.

13
CHAPTER

Mystery Woman, Etta Place

E tta Place was an enigma in her time and still is today. We know her as the woman who first went to Argentina with the Sundance Kid in 1901. Even though the Pinkertons were never able to establish her true identity, it can be done now with information and technology not available at that time.

Historians have speculated for many years that Ann Bassett of Brown's Park, Colorado, was Etta Place, but there's a conflict in the Bassett/ Place time line that appears to eliminate her as a candidate.

Ann was an intelligent, educated, and independent young lady who was also very beautiful. She could ride and shoot with the cowboys and then dress up in fancy clothes, use makeup, and flirt. [1]

An outlaw in her own right, Ann was called Queen Ann Bassett and Queen of the Rustlers. However, some locals of Brown's Park snidely called her Queen of the Bedrolls because they considered her a woman of loose morals. A cowboy once made a trip to her homestead with the idea of sharing her bed, but he found it occupied when he arrived.

Later in Bolivia, Butch Cassidy said Etta Place was the best house-keeper on the Pampas, but she was a "whore at heart." [2]

In the 1890s, rustling plagued the cattle barons of Wyoming and Colorado, but they could not get a conviction against the accused in court because the jurors were townspeople, farmers, and small ranchers, some of whom were cattle rustlers themselves.

Cattle baron Ora Haley expanded his Two Bar operation by purchasing a ranch immediately east of Brown's Park. His manager, Hi Barnard, was one of most highly regarded and knowledgeable ranch managers of the west.

The ranchers in Brown's Park were concerned that Two Bar's huge herds of cattle would meander onto their land and overgraze it, leaving little for the small ranchers to use. The Brown's Park cattlemen formed an association, and elected Ann Bassett's principle sweetheart, Matt Rash, its president.

Barnard negotiated with Rash and established a line called the Divide that Two Bar cattle were not to cross and enter Brown's Park. But of course some naturally did. Cows don't care about some invisible line. Give them a fence; that they understand.

When cows ignored the Divide, some ranchers took the trespassers as their own. Some of the Brown's Park ranchers, including Ann, would occasionally cross over the Divide and rustle Two Bar cattle.

They would butcher some and brand the calves of others with their own brand. Ann developed such hatred toward the Two Bar that she drove some of their cattle over a cliff to their death into the Green River.[3]

Unable to get convictions, the barons arranged for Bernard to offer Tom Horn, the dreaded hired killer and ex-Pinkerton detective, $500 for each rustler he exterminated.[4]

In early spring of 1900, Horn arrived in Brown's Park and introduced himself as James Hicks. Horn worked for rancher Matt Rash and gained his confidence to learn who was regularly rustling cattle. Rash knew everyone and they knew him. His own girlfriend's name came up in conversation with Horn. After a short time, Hicks left Brown's Park abruptly.

**Tom Horn, Former Pinkerton Agent Turned Hired Killer
(Internet Photo)**

Soon after Horn's departure, several cattlemen, including Rash and Isom Dart found notes on their front gates warning them to leave Brown's Park within thirty days or suffer the consequences. No one left. Rash and Dart were childhood friends in Texas and came to Colorado on a cattle drive and stayed. Dart worked at the Bassett ranch as a cook and had cared for the Bassett children since they were very young, including Ann.

Rash went to Rock Springs on July 7, 1900, and then returned home to Brown's Park. On the way to his cabin, he stopped by the Bassett ranch to see his sweetheart Ann. On July 10, his decomposing body was discovered in his cabin. He had been shot and killed along with his horse, which was tied up in front of his cabin.

Matt Rash
(Courtesy of Museum of Northwest Colorado)

Ann was grief stricken over Rash's death and accused James Hicks (Horn) of murdering him. [5]

After Rash's death Dart got a "get out of town" note, too. Dart, Billy Rash, Sam and George Bassett, and three others holed up in Dart's cabin at Summit Springs. As Dart and the others walked out of the cabin one morning, Dart was shot and killed from a distance by an unknown assassin. The boys rushed back into the cabin, barricading themselves in until nightfall when they slipped out and made it to their homes. [6]

Isom Dart
(Courtesy of Wyoming Cultural Resources)

The October 17 issue of the *Steamboat Pilot* reported on the murder of Rash and Dart and the situation in Brown's Park:

Wanted to Leave
A special from Rock Springs says: There is more trouble ahead in Brown's Park, where Matt Rash, a cattleman, and Isom Dart, a colored cowman, were murdered by the lawless which makes the park their headquarters. Yesterday a letter was found near the cabin of Dart containing a notification of speedy death for the Bassetts and Joe Davenport if they do not leave the country within sixty days....

In October 1900, the killer targeted Ann. Years later she recounted the incident in an interview published by the *Colorado Magazine* in January 1953:

I sat at a table in the living room playing solitaire. Four young boys, Carl Blair, Gail Downing, and my brothers George and Eb Bassett, were lunching in the adjoining kitchen. Suddenly, the night was shattered by blasts of gunfire. Two bullets came splintering through the door, imbedding themselves in the opposite wall, less than six inches from where I had been seated. There could be not the slightest doubt for which they were intended. I dropped to the floor and rolled under the table. The boys doused the lamp and jumped to a side window to shoot out into the night in the direction the gunfire had come.

We remained in the darkened house and speculated on why our shepherd dog had not given the alarm of a night prowler's approach: he did not bark all during the night, which was most unusual. That faithful old watchdog never barked again. He had been strangled to death by the spiteful marauder.

Cassidy and Sundance were in Brown's Park right after Rash was murdered, they were there when Dart was killed, and still there when the attempt was made on Ann's life.

Ann had to leave Brown's Park to avoid being murdered. Cassidy and Sundance told her they were going to Argentina, so she asked if she could go with them. They agreed to take her, but they were going to Fort Worth, Texas first and from there to New York and then to Argentina. Ann was to meet them in Fort Worth.

Rancher Charles Ayers tipped off the Pinkertons that Cassidy and Sundance were in Rawlins, Wyoming, on October 24, 1901. Late in the evening the following night they were at McIntosh's store in Slater, Colorado, where Sundance's friend David Gillespie worked. Gillespie was surprised to see his old friend Harry Alonzo (Sundance) whom he had not seen for three years. It was a brief but eventful reunion. Before leaving the next day, Sundance told Gillespie his traveling companion Kennaday was actually Butch Cassidy; admitted he was one of the Winnemucca bank robbers; and confided that he and Cassidy were going to South America to start a new life.

Cassidy and Sundance next went to Slater Park where J. Galloway joined them; the same Galloway that traveled to Deadwood in October 1897 to provide an alibi for the man he believed to be Sundance but was actually Harv Ray.

Butch and Sundance then went to Wolcott, Colorado, where Sundance mailed a letter to Gillespie. Cassidy and Sundance gave their horses and equipment to a couple of cowboys, then boarded a train and left. [7]

By November 1900, Will Carver, Harvey "Kid Curry" Logan, Ben "the Tall Texan" Kilpatrick, Butch, and Sundance had worked their way down to Fort Worth, Texas, for some serious celebrating with the Winnemucca and Tipton robbery money. Aside from the saloons in Hell's Half Acre, they took time to have a photograph taken in their Sunday go to meeting suits.

The Fort Worth Five

Back: Will Carver Harvey Logan
Front: Sundance Ben Kilpatrick Butch Cassidy
(Denver Public Library)

The Fort Worth Five photograph became one of the most recognized photos of the Old West. It shows not only the enigmatic Butch and Sundance and three Wild Bunch members but also how successful bandits could be in all of their finery. This picture is one of four pictures that solved the mystery of who the Sundance Kid really was.

Sundance trusted his friends and they him, but there's always one person, one false friend, one Judas. Sundance mailed a copy of the Fort Worth Five picture to his friend David Gillespie. [8] He also mailed a copy to at least one other person. One of these trusted friends gave the photograph to a Pinkerton agent.

Sundance's face was never photographed by anyone other than relatives. However, the Pinkertons tied Harry Longabaugh's name to the face. Looking for the name everywhere, even back to Pennsylvania where Harry was born, got them zip. Longabaugh was in Canada. I'm sorry, but that makes me smile—a lot. But the Pinkertons were able to use the photograph to identify the other four members of the gang.

After leaving the red-light district of Fort Worth, the gang went to Fanny Porter's brothel in San Antonio. [9]

Meanwhile, back in Brown's Park, Ann received a warning letter postmarked from Cheyenne, Wyoming, and gave it to the *Denver Post* for publication. It came from either Tom Horn or the Cattlemen's Association, which just so happened to have its headquarters in Cheyenne. The newspaper published the letter on December 20, 1900.

Outlaws Growing Bolder

The latest development in connection with the reign of terror in central and western Routt County is the publication of a warning letter to Miss Ann Bassett, who has until recently been living with her father who is postmaster in Lodore and assisting in their ranch and range work.

"Nov. 12—Anna Bassett, Lodore Colo: You are requested to leave that country for parts unknown within thirty days or you will be killed. Thirty days for your life. Committee."

The note was enclosed in a letter bearing the postmark Cheyenne, Wyo., where it was mailed Nov 15th and has just been made public by Miss Bassett who is now stopping with friends in Craig (Colorado). Had there been any vigorous effort by the authorities to hunt down the murderer of Rash and Dart, the Bassetts would have paid no attention to the warning to leave, but the indifference of the authorities and the presence of suspicious characters in that section led them to believe their lives were in danger. All except the father left the country, together with Thompson and Joe Davenport who also have been warned to go by December 12.

Ann left the county intending to go to Texas to join Sundance. In an article published January 5, 1901, the *Craig Courier* stated:

Miss Ann Bassett and her brother, Elbert, arrived in Craig last Saturday from the lower country and will visit relatives and friends for about two weeks.

On January 26, the *Craig Courier* published a second article reporting that Ann had left on the morning stagecoach for Texas, with plans to visit at Grand Junction and Denver en route. Then on February 9, the *Craig Courier* published:

Ann was in the hospital in Grand Junction with pneumonia, but it was not considered dangerous. Upon recovery, she will resume her trip to Texas.

Ann had already left Grand Junction by February 9. But her illness forced a change of plans and instead of meeting Sundance in Texas she traveled to New York City by herself to meet him there.

After celebrating in Fort Worth and San Antonio, Cassidy and Sundance left the gang in Texas, went to New York City, rented rooms at Mrs. Taylor's boarding house at 234 East 12th Street, and waited for Ann to arrive.

Pinkerton records provide the source material for Cassidy, Sundance, and Etta's movements in New York and Argentina from this point until about 1903, thanks to some Pinkerton informant.

On February 4, Cassidy purchased a watch from Tiffany's for $40.10 using the alias James Ryan, [10] This is the name of the sheriff in Sundance, Wyoming, when his friend Sundance was framed and incarcerated there.

Ann arrived sometime before February 20 and joined them at the boarding house. Sundance and Ann registered as Mr. and Mrs. Harry Place, using the surname of Harry Longabaugh's mother. [11] Sundance must have discovered the family name from Harry when they worked together in the 1880s. It's good to know that Sundance had a sense of humor since it looks as though he took every available opportunity to associate his activities with Harry Longabaugh. Kind of like carefully slipping a pin in a water filled balloon, you don't want to pop it, just drain the life out of it.

Sundance had his share of the Winnemucca robbery loot, and he wanted to deposit it safely in Buenos Aires as soon as possible.

Leaving Cassidy in New York, Sundance and Ann/Etta sailed for South America on February 20, 1901, arriving in Buenos Aires on March 23. Sundance opened an account at the London and Platte River Bank. He deposited $12,000 using the alias Harry Place and gave the upscale Hotel Europa as his address.

Sundance made another innocent mistake by writing a letter to David Gillespie and some Pinkerton informant telling them he was in Buenos Aires. [12] The informant gave this letter to a Pinkerton agent and that is how the Pinkertons learned Sundance went to Argentina

Whether through Sundance luck or good karma, after partying with the locals, eating some good food, and seeing the sights for a month, Sundance and Etta returned to New York, arriving in early May, staying ahead of the law. If the Pinkertons were heading toward Argentina they missed the proverbial boat.

They checked into Mrs. Taylor's boarding house as before, registering again as Mr. and Mrs. Harry Place. Sundance's sinus infection was bothering him so after they left New York City they went to Buffalo, New York, where he was treated at the Pierce Medical Institute.

A Pinkerton memo states that the hospital visit occurred in the summer of 1901. The memo further states, as background information, that Sundance had received a "pistol wound" in the extreme west. That, of course, would have been the leg wound he received in Cortez in 1891. While in Buffalo, Sundance and Ann had their photograph taken at the Bliss Brothers Studio.

Sundance and Etta Place (1901) Buffalo, New York
(Courtesy of the Library of Congress)

The Library of Congress has this original photograph. The Pinkertons also had a copy of the same photograph, but for some unknown reason it has a "DeYoung Studio" stamp on that frame. The DeYoung Studio was in New York City, not Buffalo.

Sundance sent a copy of this photograph to David Gillespie and the Pinkerton informant with a note identifying Ann as his new wife from Texas. [13] Aside from giving the Pinkertons his whereabouts, it is highly unlikely that Sundance and Ann were ever married since he was still married to Luzernia.

William Pinkerton wrote a memo to his brother Robert on July 31, 1902 stating: "*What a great pity we did not get the information regarding the photograph while this party was in New York. It shows how daring these men are, and while you are looking for them in the wilderness and mountains they are in the midst of society.*"

When Sundance and Etta/Ann returned west they split up, but it was still not safe for Ann to return to Brown's Park. She was in the Chickasha Indian Territory, Oklahoma, on November 8, 1901, when she wrote to her brother Elbert Bassett, who had left the danger in Brown's Park by going to school in Chillicothe, Missouri. [14]

In 1992, historian and author Doris Burton said, "It was very likely that Ann Bassett was Etta Place."

In her research, she contacted NASA employee Dr. Thomas Kyle, who performed a computer analysis comparing the Bliss Studio photograph of Etta Place with one of Ann Bassett. He concluded, with the odds of five thousand to one, that they were the same person.

Ann Bassett	Etta Place
(Denver Public Library)	(Library of Congress)

After parting from Sundance and Etta/Ann in New York City Butch returned to Texas. A Pinkerton memo states Cassidy was in Sonora, Texas, when Will Carver was killed there on April 2, 1901. Blake Graham informed the Pinkertons that in May 1901, Cassidy was near Wilcox, Arizona, on his way to Globe, Arizona, to get his mail.

Pinkerton detective Charles Siringo, who was tracking the Tipton robbers, discovered Cassidy was camped in New Mexico with eight other outlaws at what Siringo called, Robbers Roost or rendezvous, not far from Alma. He also ascertained that Cassidy was using the alias Jim Lowe.

Siringo wrote Frank Murray at the Denver office and outlined his plans to infiltrate the gang. Murray wrote back, telling Siringo that he was mistaken about Lowe stating: "He had met Lowe and Lowe *was not* Butch Cassidy. "But of course Murray knew Lowe was Cassidy having met him in Alma New Mexico and identified him there when he met with William French the year before. Siringo was ordered to sell his horse and return to Denver for a new assignment. [15]

After Cassidy left the WS he went to Colfax County, New Mexico, where he was seen with the two specially built saddle packs called Kayaks given to him by WS Ranch foreman, William French, when he left there the year before.[16]

NOTES
1. McClure, *The Bassett Women*, 12.
2. Burton, *Queen Ann Bassett*, 11, 12.
3. McClure, *The Bassett Women*, 90.
4. Kelly, *Outlaw Trail*, 355.
5. McClure, *The Bassett Women*, 80, 81.
6. Carlson, *Tom Horn: Blood on the Moon*, 121.
7. Gillespie Letter and Letter from David Gillespie, Jr. to Dan Davidson and John F. Gooldy Biography.
8. David Gillespie, Jr. Letter.
9. Kelly, *Outlaw Trail*, 281.
10. Tiffany Records.
11. Pinkerton Records.
12. John F. Gooldy, *Early History of The Little Snake River Valley*, (Wyoming: American Heritage Center, University of Wyoming) 13-14
13. Ibid.
15. Siringo, *Cowboy Detective*, 355.
16. French, *Recollections of a Western Ranchman*, 277.

14
CHAPTER

The Wagner/Malta Train Robbery

When Sundance robbed the Great Northern train between Malta and Wagner, Montana, in 1892, he came away empty handed. Nine years later, he went back to the scene of the previous crime and planned, a do over. In June 1901, Sundance, Harvey Logan, and Ben Kilpatrick rode into Malta to scout out the area. A Pinkerton informant, saloonkeeper C. W. Gardiner, recognized the outlaws and sent word to the agency but he only knew them by their aliases: Bill Longabaugh and the Roberts boys. Others in town recognized Sundance, too, and noted he had not tried to hide his identity. [1]

In the afternoon on July 3, the westbound train No. 3 stopped at Malta, where Sundance quietly boarded. Before the train reached Wagner, Sundance climbed over the engine's coal tender to the engine compartment and, at gunpoint, ordered the engineer and the fireman to stop the train near the upcoming bridge.

When the train stopped, Kilpatrick and Logan came out from under the bridge and boarded the train. Newcomer Camillo Hanks remained under the bridge tending the horses. [2] Sundance ordered the engine and express car uncoupled from the passenger cars and moved farther down the track. Logan kept the passengers covered by shooting along the sides of the cars, accidentally wounded three passengers. [3]

It took three separate dynamite blasts to open the massive safe, which also destroyed the sides and top of the express car. While his compatriots prepared the charges, Sundance chatted with the fireman about the fine art of train robbing and the excellent condition of the local hay crop. After the explosions, a horseman appeared on the ridge.

Sundance said, "I don't like the looks of that. I guess I'll take a shot at him."

"Alright, Billy," Kilpatrick responded, "but don't hit him. Hit the horse."

Sundance's shot wounded the horse, but the horseman was able to nurse the horse to Wagner and sound the alarm.[4]

The Dynamited Express Car after the Curry "Hold Up" between Malta and Wagner, Mont. July 3, 1901. "Kid" Curry's gang got away with $80,000.

Wagner Express Car
(Internet Photo)

Some of the passengers noted the marksmanship of the shooter. Factually, Sundance was the best marksman of the entire Wild Bunch gang. My family recognized his marksmanship as well. With a pistol, he could shoot birds in flight and rabbits on the run. Sundance said that he "used enough ammunition in target practice over the years; the spent cartridges would fill a room."

None of the robbers' names were Billy—or William or Bill—except for Sundance. Kilpatrick always called Sundance by his real name, not his alias. Just about all of the gang members knew Sundance's real name.

The July 3, 1901, issue of the *Great Falls Daily Tribune* referred to Sundance as *"Bill Longabaugh, the supposed leader of the gang,"* and *said he was in the train robbery "that was affected on this road, near the same place in 1892."*

The tally for this job was $ 30,000 to $50,000 in unsigned bank notes. According to author James Horan after scooping up the money, Logan looked about the car and noticed a bolt of silk. He told another bandit to "open up that sack. I'm going to take this back for the old lady."

When they were leaving, a passenger named Smith asked Logan for his Colt .44 pistol.

"What for, young fellow?" Logan asked. Smith replied, "Something to remember this event by."

Logan laughed, fired the last shot in the six-shooter, and tossed it to Smith. The robbers then left hauling a fortune with them! [5]

The outlaws stopped at a ranch and traded their worn out horses and a $100 bank note from the robbery for four of the rancher's good saddle horses. [6]

The posse trailed the robbers for several days, but the effort to capture them was futile. Some posse members said the locals helped the robbers to escape, which of course, is true.

The express company and the railroad promptly offered a staggering reward of $10,000 for the robbers, dead or alive [7]

To keep from attracting attention, the four men split up as usual, with Sundance going home to Utah. A Pinkerton memo states that Sundance "was in Vernal and Price, Utah, on his way to Baggs, Wyoming, that July. With him was Jack Egan, the saloonkeeper from Ogden," Where Cassidy, Logan, and Sundance met the previous year.

Harvey Logan was captured in Knoxville, Tennessee, on December 15. He was convicted of the Wagner robbery and sentenced to prison. After supposedly bribing a deputy, Logan escaped from the Knoxville jail on June 27, 1903.[8] He was never captured and brought to justice for any of his crimes. No one knows for sure when or where he died.

On November 5, 1901, Ben Kilpatrick and his girlfriend Laura Bullion were captured in St. Louis, Missouri. He received a fifteen-year sentence and went to prison. He was released in June 1911. While robbing a train in Sanderson, Texas, on March 13, 1912, Kilpatrick was killed when the express messenger hit him over the head with an ice mallet. [9]

Back: Jack Egan Matt Warner
Front: Matt Braffett Mod Nichols
(Courtesy of The Utah State Historical Society)

William Long was back in Fremont by October, his first visit home since leaving nearly two years earlier. While home, he got in an argument with George Morrell, Luzernia's former brother-in-law, over irrigation water. Sundance and Morrell had never been friendly and the bad blood went back to when Luzernia's first husband died in 1893 and George tried to stake a claim on Silas's homestead.

The George Morrell Family
(Courtesy of Steven Taylor)

Back in Sundance's day, the ranchers took turns using the irrigation water from the ditch to water their fields. They were assigned to take the water between certain times. If a person intentionally took the water before it was his assigned time or continued taking the water after his assigned time had expired, there was a confrontation, but generally it did not become violent. George Morrell took the water that was assigned to the Long Ranch, and this time it ended not too well for George.

The *Ogden Standard Examiner* reported in its October 24, 1901, issue:

A shooting scrape occurred at Fremont...in which George Morrell was shot in the head by Wm. Long. The wound is not considered as dangerous as the beating he got on the head with a .44-caliber after the shot. The wounded man will live, but he exhibits an ugly appearance. The trouble began over water.

The *Deseret Evening News* reported in its October 24, 1901:

In a dispute over irrigation water and ditches this morning, George Morrell was shot in the head and afterwards beaten over the head with a revolver by William Long... Morrell will most probably recover.

Dr. Elias Blackburn treated Morrell's head wound and recorded the event in his journal: *"George Morrell, badly cut had been in a fight with William Long."*

More precisely, Sundance confronted Morrell at the water diversion gate in the ditch. In the ensuing argument, Sundance drew his pistol and beat Morrell on the head with it several times, firing the pistol on the last blow. The slug grazed Morrell's skull, causing him to collapse, bloody and unconscious, to the ground.

Fearing he may have killed Morrell, Sundance went to my grandfather Jerry Jackson and told him what had happened. He also told Jackson he was not going to jail and would go to Hanksville and wait for word from Jackson telling him whether Morrell was alive or dead. He also told Jackson that he was a wanted man and he could not remain to be possibly discovered.

Had Morrell died, Sundance would have temporarily gone to Robbers Roost and from there would have gone to South America permanently.

Sundance's friend Irwin Robison happened to be driving some cattle from the summer range near Fish Lake to the winter range in the south desert near Robbers Roost, so Sundance joined him for the cattle drive.

Soon after Sundance and Robison reached the Hanksville-Robbers Roost area, they met up with Butch Cassidy. This was the first time 20-year-old Robison met Cassidy, but it would not be the last.

Irwin Robison
(Courtesy of DIann Forsyth Peck)

Meeting Cassidy made an impression on Robison, who threatened to run away from home and join the Wild Bunch. After some reflection, Robison instead made his relieved mother happy by foregoing a life in crime and marrying Sundance's stepdaughter Clara Morrell the following year. After Dutch and Sundance left the Robbers Roost area in December 1901, they met up with Ann Bassett and traveled together to New York City, checking into Mrs. Taylor's boarding house again as Mr. and Mrs. Harry Place. Cassidy used James Ryan's name, posing as Ann's brother.

They left New York in early January 1902 for Buenos Aires, Argentina where they checked into the Hotel Europa under their aliases. They stayed three weeks at the hotel and visited with the Vice Council to the American Legation, George Newberry, who was a dentist by profession but also engaged in cattle trading and land speculation. Newberry suggested the three of them homestead some land near the town of

Cholila in the Chubut Province, [10] located 1,600 miles west of Buenos Aires.

This was about the most sparsely populated, secluded land on planet earth and of course nearly everyone there spoke only Spanish.

Learning of the remoteness of Cholila had a sobering effect on the Americans, especially Ann. Cholila ranch life would not be at all like ranch life back home, where cities and towns could be reached within a few days' travel from even the most remote locations.

On the other hand, back in the United States Butch and Sundance were fugitives with a price on their heads.

Those pesky Pinkertons' persistence drove them to Argentina and if they returned to the States, the Pinkertons would have them imprisoned or killed. Back home they would have to keep running and they didn't want any more of that.

Looking at all points of view, Butch and Sundance decided to avoid a bullet and stay in Argentina as they had originally planned, even though Cholila was not the ideal place.

Ann Bassett, on the other hand, was not a wanted fugitive. She did not want to live on the frontier in Argentina. She wanted to go home to Brown's Park where she was royalty, even if it was only Queen of the Rustlers.

She had a social life with friends and family who spoke English. Ann was a strong, independent woman who knew what she wanted, and she told Sundance so. It was safe for her to return to Brown's Park, as the danger for her there had passed.

Cassidy and Sundance understood how she felt, and they accepted the fact she was returning home. They decided Sundance would accompany Ann back to the United States and then return to Argentina as soon as possible. Butch remained behind to tend to some business.

Before leaving Argentina, Sundance made a sizable withdrawal from his bank account. On March 3, 1902, Sundance and Ann boarded the *Soldier Prince,* sailing first class and arriving in New York City on April 2. On that same day, Butch applied for a homestead of more than 30,000 acres in Cholila, nearly 46 square miles of land. He used the aliases James Ryan and Harry Place on the application.

In New York City Sundance and Ann again stayed at Mrs. Taylor's boarding house.[11]

In May Both Sundance and Ann sought treatment from Dr. Weinstein, at 174 Second Avenue; Sundance for catarrh and Ann apparently for some viral infection.

The Pinkerton files include a description of them taken while they were here. Sundance was described as *"about 35 years, 5'9" in height, med complexion, brown eyes and brown hair with a bro or sandy mustache, feet small not bow legged, both feet turn in walking, face much tanned with the sun."*

Ann was described as *"age 23 or 24, med comp and med dark hair, blue or gray eyes, no marks or blemishes."*

This is the only description for Etta Place, and it matches Ann Bassett to a T.

The couple eventually headed home, with Ann returning to her beloved Brown's Park. The range war was changing in favor of the small ranchers. Tom Horn, the cattle baron's paid killer, was hanged on November 20, 1903, for killing Willie Nickel when he mistook the boy for his father.[12]

When Sundance parted from Ann, he gave her part of the Winnemucca loot. She used the cash to purchase a ranch on Douglas Mountain for $1500. [13]

Ann did what she loved: she lived in Brown's Park and raised cattle. She married Hi Bernard on April 13, 1904, and they went into the cattle business together, using her ranch as their base.

She was twenty years younger than Bernard and never really loved him. Her main incentive for the marriage was her intense hatred for Ora Haley and the Two Bar Ranch. Ann knew what Haley would do once he found out his best ranch manager had married her—he fired Bernard.[14]

Bernard eventually confessed to Ann that he had hired Tom Horn to kill Matt Rash and Isom Dart, paying Horn a $1000 for the two killings. [15] Hell has no fury like a woman wounded from the loss of her best friend and love, Matt Rash. And Dart had cared for her from cradle to womanhood.

So after a total of eight years of marriage, Ann Bassett divorced Hi Bernard.

NOTES
1. *Anaconda Standard,* July 14, 1901.
2. Kelly, *Outlaw Trail,* 282, 283.
3. *Anaconda Standard,* July 14, 1901.
4. *Great Falls Daily Tribune,* July 4, 1901.
5. Horan, *Desperate Men,* 214.
6. Patterson, *Butch Cassidy, a Biography,* 191.
7. *Anaconda Standard* August 14, 1901.
8. Kelly, *Outlaw Trail,* 285..
9. Kelly, *Outlaw Trail,* 307.
10. Daimio's Pinkerton report.
11. Ibid.
12. Carlson, *Blood on the Moon,* 299.
13. McClure, *The Bassett Women,* 90.
14. Ibid., 90–93
15. Kelly, *Outlaw Trail,* 355.

15
CHAPTER

Etta #2; Butch and Sundance's False Demise

For many years I, like many others, believed Ann Bassett was Etta Place, but there was a conflict in the time lines I could not reconcile. Solve one mystery and another one pops up.

In July 1902, a woman identified as Etta Place went with Sundance to Argentina and remained there for several years.[1] But Ann purchased a ranch in Brown's Park in late 1902 or 1903, and she married Hi Bernard in 1904. Except for the time she was with Sundance in New York and Buenos Aires, Argentina, her life is well documented so that appeared to eliminate Ann Bassett from being Etta Place; or at least, from being the only Etta Place. I concluded there was a second woman also identified as Etta Place.

Like Ann, she had to be someone Sundance knew well, and someone probably associated with the outlaws from Wayne County and the Robbers Roost. I believe this second Etta was outlaw Jack Moore's common law widow.

Author Pearl Baker asserts, "Her name was Nora, and she was Monte Butler's sister."

Charles Kelly said her name was Ella. The court records refer to her only as Mrs. Jack Moore.

Whatever her name was, the evidence points to Moore's widow as being the second Etta.

Jack Moore was a Texas cowboy that first arrived in the Robbers Roost area in the 1880s. Aside from being the foreman at the Granite Ranch "where outlaws were welcome," Moore stole livestock and took them to markets around Telluride.

Moore eventually sent for his wife Nora and the couple were invited to live at the ranch house. Nora's primary responsibility was to care for ranch owner J.B. Buhr. His chronic asthma earned him the nickname Wheezing Buhr.

Buhr grew up in Denver, where he had been a tailor, and he delighted in making Nora fancy riding costumes. If Ann Bassett was Queen of the Rustlers in Brown's Park, then the beautiful Nora Moore was Queen of the Outlaws in Robbers Roost. Pearl Baker describes Nora as: *"cultured and pleasant, she had good taste, and softened the cabin with pictures, sofa pillows, and other luxuries. She wouldn't let the cowboys smoke or swear in the house, but they didn't seem to resent it. They ate their meals in the kitchen and sat in the parlor to read and visit."*[2]

Kelly said in his book, "She was a guiding influence among the rustlers." [3]

On one of Moore's rustling trips he went to Placerville, Colorado, where his brother-in-law Monte Butler lived. He invited Butler to join him at the Robbers Roost and "jump in on rustling some cattle." Butler went with Moore and brought his wife Ella along. At a layover, they inscribed their names into a rock wall at Water Hole Flats near Robbers Roost.

Butler Inscriptions
Monte Butler   Ella Butler
(Authors' Collection)

It wasn't long before Monte and Ella met Butch Cassidy and was invited to join Cassidy and Elza Lay when they set up camp in Horseshoe Canyon after they robbed the Castle Gate payroll in April 1897.

In May 1898, Moore was shot and killed by a rancher in Baggs, Wyoming, while trying to steal horses.[4] After Moore's death, Nora continued to live at the Granite Ranch and to care for Wheezing Buhr.

On June 6, 1899, Buhr and Nora were arrested and charged with harboring criminals. They were tried in nearby Hanksville but charges were discharged after Buhr bought the jury a keg of beer.[5]

Soon after their acquittal, Nora and Buhr gathered up his horses and left Robbers Roost. I'm not certain where and when Sundance first met Nora, but it's logical to assume Butch had introduced them at Robbers Roost area in 1897. However they met, Sundance knew her circumstances when she left the Granite Ranch, and knew exactly where she went and how to contact her, which he did.

With Ann Bassett safely back in Brown's Park, Sundance invited Nora to travel with him to meet Butch at their ranch in Argentina.

Ann Bassett was not willing to live on the frontier in Argentina but Nora was. Nora knew horses and could ride and shoot like a cowboy. She was comfortable in the company of outlaws, and had been arrested herself for harboring outlaws. She knew what she was getting into and was willing to go.

Somewhere in the Robbers Roost or Denver area, Nora met up with Sundance for the journey to Argentina. They were in New York City by June 25, 1902, where Sundance purchased her a watch from Tiffany's for $15.35. [6] They traveled as Mr. and Mrs. Harry A. Place, as he had with Ann.

On July 10, 1902, they left New York aboard the ship *Honorius*, arriving in Buenos Aires on August 9 and checking into the Hotel Europa. On August 14, Sundance withdrew his remaining $1,105.50 from the London and Platt River Bank and closed the account. On August 15 they sailed from Buenos Aires to Madryn, Argentina, and then traveled by horseback to the ranch.

On his way to the ranch, Cassidy went through the town of Trelew, Argentina, where he withdrew $3,546 from Sundance's bank account to buy livestock and supplies. Cassidy settled into ranch life but apparently became very lonely.

On August 10, he wrote the following letter to his friend Mathilda Davis in Utah:

"I suppose you have thought long before this that I have forgotten you (or was dead), but my dear friend I am still alive.... It will probably surprise you to hear from me away down in this country, but the U.S. was too small for me. The last two years I was there, I was restless. I wanted to see more of the world. I had seen all of the U.S. that I thought was good.... Another of my uncles died and left $30,000 to our little family of three [Obviously, this is a reference to Cassidy, Sundance, and Will Carver robbing the Winnemucca, Nevada, bank on Sept 19, 1900.]; so I took my $10,000 and started to see a little more of the world. I visited the best cities and best parts of country of South A. till I got here,

and this part of the country looked so good that I located, and I think for good, for I like the place better every day…. I am still living in single cussedness, and I sometimes feel very lonely, for I am alone all day, and my neighbors don't amount to anything. Besides, the only language spoken in this country is Spanish, and I don't speak it well enough yet to converse in the latest scandals so dear to the hearts of all nations, and without which conversations are very stale, but the country is first class. The only industry at present is stock raising (that is in this part), and it can't be beat for that purpose, for I have never seen a finer grass country…I am a long way from civilization." [7]

When Sundance and Nora arrived at the ranch, the reunion with Cassidy cheered them all up.

There is no record of Cassidy returning to the United States after he first arrived in Argentina in 1902 until his permanent return in 1907 or 1908. Sundance, on the other hand, made at least three return trips. Sundance had a family in Fremont, whereas Cassidy did not have a wife or children in the United States.

A Pinkerton memo states that in 1903 Sundance returned to the United States but it does not give the reason. [8] During his visit to Fremont on that trip Sundance agreed to purchase 9.75 acres of land from Mary Palmer for $300. The county clerk, William J. Grundy, executed the warranty deed on October 16, 1903. The deed shows: "Signed in the presence of Luzernia Long, Wm Grundy, and Mary Palmer."

William Long's signature is conspicuously absent. [9] He made the agreement to purchase the property and paid for it, but he left before it was recorded with the county clerk. Sundance was back at the ranch in Cholila, Argentina, before the end of 1904.

Cassidy and Sundance believed they were safe from the Pinkertons on the Argentinean frontier but because of the letter Sundance sent to a Pinkerton informant in March 1901, from Buenos Aires they were mistaken. The Pinkertons sent agent Frank Dimaio to investigate in March

1903. Dimaio discovered when Sundance and Etta Place had sailed from New York to Buenos Aires as well as the bank where Sundance deposited his money.

When the detective showed the bank manager photographs of Butch, Sundance, and Etta/Ann, he recognized them. Dimaio also discovered they had established a ranch in Cholila. Before leaving Argentina, he had circulars printed and distributed with their descriptions, photographs, and rewards offered for their capture. The circulars also had the picture of Etta/Ann Bassett that was taken at the Bliss Brothers studio in Buffalo in 1901. [10] These circulars would eventually catch up with them.

In 1905, a former sheriff's deputy from the United States happened to become one of their neighboring landowners. He recognized the men and reported them to authorities for the reward, I'm sure. This discovery must have devastated Cassidy. Even on the frontier in Argentina, he could not escape the possibility that the Pinkertons would find them.

Knowing they had been discovered, Cassidy went to Chile and sold the ranch to a local organization. [11]

Cassidy and Sundance knew they had been discovered and their supernatural instincts told them it was time to run, yet again. They must have thought it was hopeless to settle down and live a peaceful life in obscurity.

After they sold the ranch in 1905, Sundance and Nora returned to the States for another visit, but this time they departed from the west coast of South America at Antofagasta, Chile. A Pinkerton memo dated January 26, 1906, reports that Sundance had some unnamed difficulty with the Chilean government in Antofagasta and with the help of U.S. vice counsel Frank Aller settled the matter for a tidy sum of $1,500.

It was almost inevitable that they returned to what they knew and robbed a bank. On March 2, 1906, Butch, Sundance, Nora, and Harvey Logan who, according to the Pinkerton files, had traveled to

Argentina to join Cassidy and Sundance, held up the bank of Nacion Villa Mercedes in San Luis, Argentina.

During the robbery the bank manager entered the room to see what was happening and sounded the alarm. He was shot in the head and instantly killed, probably by Harvey Logan. Making a hasty exit they mounted their horses and galloped away. A posse was immediately formed and the robbers were almost overtaken before they could reach their relay horses. Telling the others to go ahead, Butch dismounted with his rifle and winged one man and killed two horses. After that, the posse turned back.

Butch caught up to the others and with fresh horses, the gang made their escape. [12] After the robbery, Nora decided that she'd had enough of South America. She had been forced to give up their life at the ranch in Cholila because of the Pinkertons' reward. She helped commit a bank holdup and was now a fugitive on the run.

Nora wanted to take her share of the loot, return to the United States, and live comfortably for a while.

Sundance and Nora sailed back to the United States via Antofagasta, Chile, again. After leaving Nora at a Denver hospital, Sundance checked into a boarding house, got drunk, and shot holes into the ceiling. When the landlady called the police, Sundance left. [13]

Our family believes that Sundance had a son with a mistress. Maybe Nora's hospital visit was for the birth of that son. I have not been able to verify that either way.

Leaving Denver, Sundance visited his family in Fremont and bought four more acres of land from H. E. and Ruth Maxfield for $50. A warranty deed was recorded on January 17, 1907, with ownership conveyed to William Long and notarized by John Curfew. The only persons present at the signing were H.E. Maxfield and John Curfew. [14] Once again, Sundance had already returned to South America when this warrant deed was recorded.

Before he left for South America, Sundance went to Fish Lake and stashed some of the loot from the bank robbery in Argentina.

In late 1906, Sundance met Roy Letson, who was buying mules for a railroad the Bolivian government was constructing. Letson hired Sundance as a muleteer, which eventually took him to the Concordia Tin Mine in Bolivia.

Sundance made an agreement with mine manager Rolla Glass to work there. A short time later Cassidy, using the alias Santiago Maxwell, also came to work at the mine as a muleteer. Sundance used the name Enrique Brown.

Butch and Sundance developed a friendship with Percy Seibert, who took over from Rolla Glass as manager.

Most of the stories about Cassidy and Sundance in South America came from Seibert, who later became acquainted with journalist Arthur Chapman. Chapman found Seibert's stories about his association with the outlaws so interesting he published a compilation in the April 1930 issue of the *Elks* magazine titled *"Butch Cassidy."*

Seibert told Chapman he came to like the bandits, especially Cassidy, who he found to be pleasant, cultured, and charming. He considered him an excellent and trustworthy employee. Seibert assigned Cassidy to carry the payroll and to purchase livestock and supplies for the mine.

Glass and Seibert discovered they were wanted outlaws by seeing the Pinkerton wanted posters somewhere in their travels. When confronted, Cassidy told Glass, they didn't "rob people they worked for," and they were kept on at the mine. [15]

Cassidy told Seibert that when they first came to South America, they intended to be law abiding ranchers, but a neighbor at Cholila Ranch had recognized them and told the authorities, hoping to collect the reward for their capture. Cassidy did not realize that the Pinkertons had found them by acquiring the letter Sundance sent to the Pinkerton informant from Buenos Aires in 1901.

Cassidy added: "There's no use trying to hide and go straight. There's always an informer around to bring the law on you. After you've started, you have to keep going, that's all. The safest way is to keep moving all the time and spring a holdup in some new place. In that way, you keep the other fellows guessing."[16]

They gave Seibert a demonstration of their shooting ability by throwing beer bottles in the air and shooting them with a pistol. [17]

Seibert was more at ease with Cassidy than Sundance, who he found distant and sullen, making it difficult to strike up a friendship.[18] When Sundance was with his family in Utah, he was just the opposite. At this point, Sundance was homesick and wanted to return home to his family.

Sundance told Seibert he was from New Jersey and that his sister had married a congressman. This of course is complete bison bull. He also told Seibert he had run away from home to become a cowboy "after reading some thrilling novels of the West." [19] That story does have a ring of truth. Viola's 1937 letter states he ran away from home to a cowboy camp when he was a boy of six years old.

When it became widely known by the workers that Butch and Sundance were wanted bandits, the two men settled their account and left, not wanting to cause any problems for the mine or Seibert. A short time later they held up the remittance coach of the San Domingo Mine in Peru and the Bolivia Railway pay train at Eucalyptus, Bolivia. [20]

They'd had enough of South America and the outlaw life. Butch was 40 and Sundance was 45 years old. When you think about it, that's pretty old for robbing banks on horseback and messing around getting shot at but in today's world, they were youngsters.

Except for Sundance's brief visits back home, they had been gone seven or eight years. They both wanted to return home and live in obscurity. They had the loot from the last three or four holdups and the sale of the ranch. With it, they could live comfortably for quite a while.

Sundance had to take care of some unnamed last minute business before leaving so they agreed to meet at a designated place. Cassidy never made the rendezvous because his leg became badly swollen from a scorpion bite and they lost track of each other.

Cassidy was nursed back to health by a local Indian woman and then left South America alone and for good. Sundance remained for a while longer.[21] They never saw each other again until seventeen years later back in Utah.

On an isolated Bolivian trail on November 4, 1908, two American bandits robbed an Aramayo Mining Company official of the mine's pay-roll. Unlike a well-planned Butch Cassidy robbery, the bandits remained in the area. You know that's an amateur's mistake; Butch and Sundance rode as fast as they could to get many miles between them and the scene of a robbery.

On November 7, these two amateur bandits rode into the nearby town of San Vicente, thirty miles from the robbery scene and rented a room for the night. A local person became suspicious and sent word to a nearby Bolivian Army patrol.

A few soldiers went to San Vicente to investigate. With two or three soldiers and the sheriff, they confronted the bandits. A few shots were exchanged and a soldier was killed. The bandits were ordered to surrender, but they refused. A serious gun battle ensued, which lasted half an hour before the bandits were killed. The soldiers found the two dead bandits in the room. Almost the entire payroll was recovered.[22]

Even though Sundance was still in Bolivia or Chile, both Butch's sister Lula Bentenson and some Pinkerton letters confirm that Cassidy had returned to the United States before the November 4 1908, robbery. Both Bentenson and the Pinkerton letters also confirm he was still in the United States after the Bandits were killed in San Vicente. The letters show that former United States Marshall Frank A. Hadsell informed the Pinkerton Denver office that Cassidy was in Evanston, Wyoming, on May 26 and again on May 31, 1908.

Wells Fargo agent F. J. Dodge informed the Pinkertons that Cassidy was in the vicinity of Price and Cisco, Utah, the last part of February 1909. He further informed them that Cassidy was also in the Henry Mountains the last part of February 1909, with Gunplay Maxwell and Tom McCarty. These mountains are near Hanksville and are considered to be in the Robbers Roost. And then Dodge said that Cassidy was with a man named "Hall" at Woodside Utah, on March 1, 1909.

The following letters are mangled but readable.

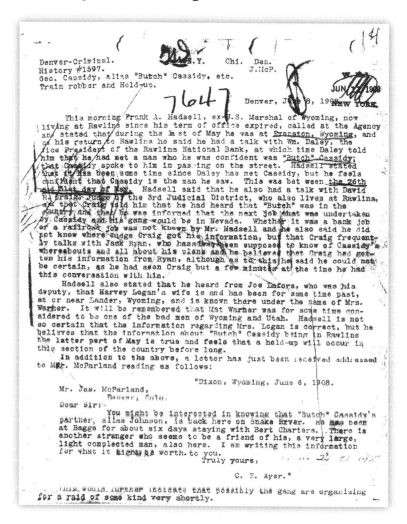

Denver-Criminal.
History #1597.
Geo. Cassidy, alias "Butch" Cassidy, etc.
Train robber and Hold-up.

N.Y. Chi. Den.
J.McP.

Denver, June 8, 1908

This morning Frank A. Hadsell, ex-U.S. Marshal of Wyoming, now living at Rawlins since his term of office expired, called at the Agency and stated that during the last of May he was at Evanston, Wyoming, and on his return to Rawlins he said he had a talk with Wm. Daley, the Vice President of the Rawlins National Bank, at which time Daley told him that he had met a man who he was confident was "Butch" Cassidy; that Cassidy spoke to him in passing on the street. Hadsell stated that it has been some time since Daley has met Cassidy, but he feels confident that Cassidy is the man he saw. This was between the 26th and 31st day of May. Hadsell said that he also had a talk with David H. Craig, Judge of the 3rd Judicial District, who also lives at Rawlins, and that Craig told him that he had heard that "Butch" was in the country and that he was informed that the next job that was undertaken by Cassidy and his gang would be in Nevada. Whether it was a bank job or a railroad job was not known by Mr. Hadsell and he also said he did not know where Judge Craig got his information, but that Craig frequently talks with Jack Ryan, who has always been supposed to know of Cassidy's whereabouts and all about his plans and he believed that Craig had gotten his information from Ryan, although as to this he said he could not be certain, as he had seen Craig but a few minutes at the time he had this conversation with him.

Hadsell also stated that he heard from Joe Lefors, who was his deputy, that Harvey Logan's wife is and has been for some time past, at or near Lander, Wyoming, and is known there under the name of Mrs. Warner. It will be remembered that Mat Warner was for some time considered to be one of the bad men of Wyoming and Utah. Hadsell is not so certain that the information regarding Mrs. Logan is correct, but he believes that the information about "Butch" Cassidy being in Rawlins the latter part of May is true and feels that a hold-up will occur in this section of the country before long.

In addition to the above, a letter has just been received addressed to Mr. McParland reading as follows:

"Dixon, Wyoming, June 6, 1908.

Mr. Jas. McParland,
Denver, Colo.

Dear Sir:

You might be interested in knowing that "Butch" Cassidy's partner, alias Johnson, is back here on Snake River. He has been at Baggs for about six days staying with Bert Charters. There is another stranger who seems to be a friend of his, a very large, light complected man, also here. I am writing this information for what it might be worth to you.

Truly yours,

C. E. Ayer."

This would further indicate that possibly the gang are organizing for a raid of some kind very shortly.

Pinkerton File

Chicago-Criminal.   N.Y.
History No. 3545.
George Parker, alias Geo. Cassidy.
                     Thos. Cassidy.
                     Butch Cassidy.
                     George Ingerfield.

                                        Chicago, March 22nd, 1900.

      James McParland, Esq.,

           .I.F. Manager, Denver.

      Dear Sir:-

                On March 6th, F. J. Dodge, Special Officer of the Wells,
      Fargo Express Co., wrote Principal William A. Pinkerton from Raton,
      New Mexico, as follows:

                "I would thank you to furnish me a history of Butch
           Cassidy also a photo if you have one. I am very much
           afraid that we are going to hear from the gentleman in
           an unpleasant way in the near future. My memorandum on
           him is somewhat meager. I am up against a hard game
           here. I know my man and have an abundance of evidence
           but the situation in the courts here is something awful."

                We forwarded him a circular enclosing photograph and des-
      cription of "Butch Cassidy" and requested him to write us further
      particulars. Under date of March 18th, Mr. Dodge, writes to
      Principal William A. Pinkerton as follows:

                "Your letter of the 12th inst. with circular of Cassidy
           and Longbaugh enclosed, reached me here and I will send
           the circular to parties that I have looking into this
           matter.
                I received some information about the last of Feb.
           that Butch Cassidy had been seen in the vicinity of Price
           and Cisco, Utah, and he was in company with a fellow
           called "Gun-play" Maxwell and Tom McCarty, and they were
           located in the Henry Mountains, where it is claimed that
           Maxwell has a Placer Claim, and later Butch Cassidy was
           seen in company with a man by the name of Hall. They
           were seen together at Woodside, Utah about the 1st of
           March. Maxwell and Tom McCarty were still in the Henry
           Mountains. The Henry Mountains are about 75 miles south
           of Green River. I feel pretty sure that this information
           is correct and I would not wonder if they were arranging
           to give us a touch of high life there as soon as the
           weather gets mild enough for them to travel well.
                I will give you any information that I may be able to
           obtain and I will also write our Superintendent in Denver to
           furnish you direct with anything that he gets in regard to
           this party."

Pinkerton Files

150

Pinkerton Files
(Courtesy Library of Congress)

Sundance was still in Chile and he wanted the Pinkertons to believe that he and Cassidy were the two dead robbers. If death certificates could be obtained identifying them as the dead robbers, perhaps the Pinkertons would accept it as fact, close the case forever, and Sundance could kick the South American dust off his boots and go home to Utah.

Their friend and former employer Siebert from the tin mine did what he could to help. He said the two bandits were Butch and Sundance, even though Seibert never saw the bandits' bodies. Having a friend pays off, big time!

Four years earlier, Sundance had paid United States Vice Consul Frank Aller $1,500 to help him out of some difficulty with the Chilean government. Once again he asked Aller to help, presumably for another fee.

On July 31, 1909, Frank Aller sent a request to the American Legation in La Paz, Bolivia, for death certificates of the robbers killed in San Vicente and buried as unknowns.

Apparently, his original letter was lost, so Aller sent a second request to Alexander Benson at the American Legation. In September 1910, Benson sent Aller a copy of the request he had made to the Bolivian Minister of Foreign Affairs. The letter referred to Sundance and Cassidy's aliases, Brown and Maxwell respectively, as the deceased.

Benson wrote that a Chilean judge "wants legal proof of their death, in order to settle the estate." There were no estate assets; they were bandits. Benson went on to say, "Brown and Maxwell were the men who held up several of the Bolivian Railway Company's pay trains and also the stagecoaches of several mines, and I understand were killed in a fight with soldiers who were detached to capture them as outlaws."

The Bolivian government would not issue death certificates naming the dead bandits as Brown and Maxwell. They said the robbers were unknown. Even though Aller failed to get the death certificates, he recorded in United States documents that they were killed. [23]

The Pinkertons, however, never closed the case. They knew Cassidy had been in the United States before and after the Bolivian robbery.

Luck, by definition, is a force that operates for good; a combination of circumstances or events that result in success. Butch Cassidy and the Sundance Kid's lifelong, tremendously fortunate good luck once again favored them to the max. Even though the Pinkertons didn't buy into their Bolivian demise, they seemed content to let the fiction stand.

In 1912, Cassidy visited Robbers Roost and while there, he engraved "1912" into a rock that he had previously engraved his name into in the 1890s. [24] It's possible he visited Sundance In Fremont but I just don't know for sure.

On this visit he became sick, probably with the flu, and was unable to continue. So Butch stopped at Irwin Robison's Trachyte Ranch to recover his health. Robison nursed him back to health and cared for his horse. When Cassidy recovered, he insisted Robison accept his 30-30 Winchester rifle as payment. He told Robison he might be back later to pay for his kindness and get the rifle, but Cassidy never returned, and the rifle is still owned by Robison's descendants.

**Etta Robinson Forsyth with Butch Cassidy's Winchester Riffle
(Authors' Collection)**

In 1925 Butch returned to Circleville to visit his family. This was the first visit home in many, many years. He drove up in a new Ford and at first; his father Max didn't recognize him. His younger sister Lula was called, and when she arrived, she did not recognize him either. She said he looked familiar and was not a stranger, and yet he was. Max said, "Lula this is Leroy." Lula said any resentment she had toward her outlaw brother melted; the prodigal had returned!

They reminisced about the wonderful old times they enjoyed, and he also expressed deep sorrow for breaking his mother's heart.

Cassidy said his life had been wasted and explained his desire to go straight and his inability to escape his past, and how he never quit paying the price. He shared his frustration at how the meeting with the railroad executives at loss Soldier Pass was never consummated. He also said he was forever grateful to Siebert for identifying him as one of the dead bandits.

He told them the last time he saw Sundance was in South America. "Sundance went to take care of last minute business. We were to meet at a certain place, but my leg was so bad, as a result of a scorpion bite, I couldn't keep the appointment."

Butch described some of his trips over the years. "I traveled a lot in Europe, especially Spain, also Italy. Italians were very warm and friendly people, and I loved them."

When he left Circleville, he told them he was going to travel around and see some old friends. [25] He would soon visit my grandparents in Fremont and Sundance at Matt Warner's saloon in Price.

Butch Cassidy and the Sundance Kid disappeared from the bandit life and became obscure, a mystery inside an enigma, almost lost to history, almost lost completely...but not quite!

NOTES
1. Pinkerton records.
2. Baker, *The Wild Bunch at Robbers Roost,* 40–41.
3. Kelly, *Outlaw Trail,*148
4 Baker, *The Wild Bunch at Robbers Roost,* 44–45).
5. Kelly, *Outlaw Trail,* 222.
6. Tiffany Records.
7. Warner, *Last of the Bandit Riders,* 166.
8. Pinkerton Memo dated January, 26, 1906.
9. Wayne County, Utah Land Records.
10. Dimaio Pinkerton report.
11. Arthur Chapman, "Butch' Cassidy, " *Elks Magazine,* April 1930.
12. ibid
13. Ibid.
14. Wayne County, Utah Land Records.
15. Chapman, *Butch Cassidy.*
16. ibid.
17. Ernst, *The Sundance Kid,* 160.
18. Chapman, *Butch Cassidy.*
19. Meadows, *Digging Up Butch and Sundance,* 96.
20. Chapman, *Butch Cassidy.*
21. Betenson, *Butch Cassidy My Brother, 182-183.*
22. Patterson, *Butch Cassidy a Biography,* 215-216.
23. Meadows, *Digging Up Butch and Sundance,* 127, 128.
24. Baker, *The Wild Bunch at Robbers Roost,* 210
25. Betenson, *Butch Cassidy, My Brother,* 179–188.

16
CHAPTER

The Quiet Years

During the time Sundance was In South America, Luzernia and his daughters were living on the original Morrell homestead in Fremont. Around 1904, Luzernia's oldest daughter Chloe, her husband Jerry Jackson, and their family moved in to help Luzernia run the homestead. Luzernia's second daughter, Clara, and her husband Irwin Robison lived nearby in Loa.

Sundance had been gone so long that when he returned, he was a virtual stranger to his daughters who had seen him only a few, brief times in ten years. He moved Luzernia and their two daughters Viola and Evinda out of the original homestead house and built a new, smaller house in Fremont about a mile away. Jerry and Chloe Jackson inherited the original homestead house with ten acres.

Evinda and Viola Long
(Courtesy of Gaylen Robison)

Most of the Fremont stories come from the Jackson and the Robison families. People remembered that Sundance liked to dress well, had the best horses, and the fanciest saddle and riding gear around. He never had a steady job but always had pocket money, and the family often wondered where he got it. I suspect that Luzernia knew it came from nefarious sources but not necessarily what exactly.

Sundance also had a cabin in the Danish Meadow in the mountains above Fremont. If ever he thought there was danger, he would go to this cabin and stay until he felt safe. To this day, the Meadow is only accessible by horseback or off road vehicles. The trail to the meadow is not marked so if you are not familiar with it you can't find it.

Sundance never told the family that he went to South America or that he was the Sundance Kid. Makes one wonder what exactly he did tell them. All the family knew was that he was gone for long periods of time and then returned home.

They knew he had been an outlaw that rode with Butch Cassidy, and people guessed which bandit he might be. Some believed he was Bill McCarty, but McCarty was killed in 1893.

Sundance's daughter Viola and others did not believe he was McCarty. They searched but never discovered from where he came or his lineage. When they studied the Fort Worth Five photo and recognized him as the person identified as Harry Longabaugh, they concluded it could not possibly be their father because that person was Harry Longabaugh and their father was William Long.

Besides, they believed Harry Longabaugh was married to Etta Place, and their father was always happily married to their mother Luzernia. Perhaps they did not want to admit that the picture they saw was their dad because that meant he was a killer and bandit and, maybe worse, cheated on their mother. Generations removed, I'm disappointed that he ran around with other women too.

While living in Fremont and tending the homestead, Sundance also had other jobs. Between 1912 and 1915 he worked for his step son in law Irwin Robison clearing the ground and making irrigation ditches for $3 a day at Robison's Trachyte ranch.

Robison's Trachyte Ranch
(Courtesy of Barbara Ekker)

In 1913, Robison was elected sheriff of Wayne County. His father Alvin Robison was the county judge. I think both Robisons knew that William Long was an outlaw but wouldn't turn him in anyway because he was family.

Since Robison wasn't a gunman and the sheriff needed to know how to draw and shoot, he often took target practice with Sundance, who gave him pointers on how to use a pistol.

They would drive a large nail into an old shed and practice shooting along the side of the shed at the head of the nail from a reasonable distance away. Sundance could pull and shoot one shot and the nail would be gone.

Robison resigned as sheriff in 1915 because he could not take care of his ranch and handle the job as sheriff, too.

Sundance would occasionally give glimpses into his old life. He was once riding with his grandson Ray Jackson near Fremont. When they rode past a particular tree, Sundance pointed and said, "That's where we hung that SOB." Ray asked what he was talking about, but Sundance just said, "Never mind!"

Another time, my mother Luzernia Jackson and Evinda, the second daughter of Sundance and Luzernia were playing. They caught a grasshopper and put it in a matchbox and named it "Butch Cassidy." When Sundance heard them, he told them "never say or use that name again!"

Sundance told his grandson Perry Jackson, "If you isn't a good shot, then you're a dead shot."

He taught his grandsons how to be crack shots by saying, "Just lay your finger alongside the barrel of a six shooter, and then when you point your finger, you'll be right on target."

While living in Fremont, Luzernia helped support the family by raising turkeys and selling or trading them to the local store or to neighbors. Later, a trader from Salt Lake City bought her turkeys.

Sundance and Luzernia enjoyed the company of her many family members who lived relatively close. They would all get together for Sunday dinner.

Sundance (Bearded Man on Right) Luzernia (With Bonnet)
(Courtesy of Diann Forsyth Peck)

Although he lived peacefully in Fremont, Sundance seemed to enjoy antagonizing the county game warden. Like the time Sundance was fishing illegally out of season at Seven-Mile Creek near Fish Lake and noticed in the distance the game warden coming toward him.

**Looking Across Fish Lake at Skougarrd Lodge, 2010
(Authors' Collection)**

Sundance mounted his horse and rode up the trail to a friend's cabin. Laughing the entire time, they pushed his horse inside the cabin and then sat in the front yard and calmly waited. When the warden arrived, he asked the two if they had seen a man ride by. Both men said yes, pointed toward the trail, and the game warden took off after his man.

On another occasion, Sundance took his teenage grandsons Raymond and Thomas Jackson fishing just below the dam at Forsyth Reservoir. He illegally shut the water gate off stranding the fish in the creek bed below the dam. He told Ray and Tom to gather the fish by hand while he stood guard. As the boys were gathering the fish, the game warden came crawling along the creek bank on his hands and knees with intensions of catching the culprits. From his lookout point, Sundance shot into the sand in front of the game warden who quickly left the scene. When the boys heard the shot, they came running and asked what he was shooting at. "A varmint," Sundance said. "Let's go look." They found the bullet had hit between the warden's handprints in the sand. Sundance had done almost the same thing to the old man in Winnemucca, Nevada, by shooting between his feet when the gang robbed the bank there.

Jackson Family
Standing L–R: (My mother) Luzernia Raymond Thomas Harvey Eleanor
Middle Row: Jerry Worthen Chloe
Front: Chloe
(Courtesy of Viola Jackson Buchanan)

Another time, he was pretending to be fishing in the closed waters at the Fish Hatchery in Fremont. The warden saw him and was on his way to give him a ticket. When Sundance saw the game warden coming, he mounted his horse and rode off. He pretended his horse had pulled up lame and stopped, allowing the game warden to catch him. "I caught you red handed this time, Bill," the game warden said, and demanded Sundance hand over the fish that were wrapped in a blanket behind his saddle. But when the warden opened the bundle, he discovered sticks, not fish. Looking up, he saw Sundance, with a threatening look demanding he wrap the sticks back just like he found them, which he did quickly.

Around 1913, Sundance and his son-in-law Swearing Charlie Anderson got drunk, broke into the Skougrarrd Resort at Fish Lake, and shot the keys off the piano with pistols.

Skougaard Lodge at Fish Lake
(Authors' Collection)

They were caught and the sheriff told Bill he would have to pay $90 for the damages. Sundance later said it was the most expensive piano lesson he ever took.

Mary and "Swearing" Charlie Anderson
(Courtesy of Diann Forsyth Peck)

While roping cattle one day at Charlie Anderson's place, Sundance got his right thumb tangled in the rope; with 400 to 600 pounds of cow on the pulling end of the rope against one little thumb, the cow won and pulled off Sundance's thumb. That night, he put the thumb on a shelf to see if the doctor could sew it on the following day. The next morning he discovered that a mouse had gnawed on the thumb, so he had it buried that day.

**Sundance and Luzernia in Their Late Sixties;
Note His Missing Right Thumb
(Authors' Collection)**

Another time, a neighbor in Fremont had a very good horse that Sundance wanted so he offered to buy it but the neighbor did not want to sell the animal. When the owner went to the corral the next day the horse was gone but there was a Prince Albert tobacco can nailed to the gatepost filled with money.

Ironically, Sundance once said, "Never ride a good, fast horse into an outlaw camp because you won't get it back."

Sundance remained reliant on horses all his life. The bronco busting world traveler, gun-slinging bandit with little or no fear refused to learn to drive an automobile. But, he had a buggy and a team of horses he was very proud of.

By 1916, the original Morrell homestead in Fremont had been divided and sold off or given to descendants. Sundance and Luzernia sold the remaining 10 acres and moved to Duchesne, Utah, to be near their daughter Evinda who had married a man from that area. When they found a ranch they wanted to buy, Sundance left Duchesne for two weeks and returned with at least $1,700 in cash, which he used to buy the ranch. It was said he had some loot stashed near Fish Lake and returned there to get it. This most likely was part of the loot from the Banco de la Nacion Bank robbery of 1906.

Sundance and Luzernia lived out the remainder of their lives on this ranch. In the winter time, they would live with their daughter Viola wherever she was.

Sundance and Luzernia's Duchesne Home Today
(Authors' Collection)

Sundance and Luzernia lived happily on the farm in Duchesne, and many of their descendants live in the area to this day. By the time they moved to Duchesne, Sundance no longer provoked game wardens or anyone else. He lived quietly and got along well with his neighbors.

But Sundance still had one fault that caused Luzernia pain; he was a handsome man with a charismatic personality that women found attractive. He had at least one affair and perhaps more. When he left home to see his lady friend, Luzernia would pull her apron up over her head so no one could see her face. But everything else about him demonstrated that he was a loving and loved husband, father, and grandfather.

Viola's daughter and Sundance's granddaughter, Elva, said, "I just can't believe he was an outlaw." Many of the people who knew him have the same opinion. Elva remembers him rocking her as a child and singing "In the Good Old Summertime" to her.

She remembers one time when she and her younger brother stopped to play with the neighboring children instead of going straight home after school. Soon they saw their Grandpa Long coming down the road for them with a switch in his hand. They stopped playing and went home with grandpa following them, flipping the switch. Elva would later laugh about it because she knew he would "never" spank any of his grandchildren. I believe you can see a man's true worth in how he treats his children and grandchildren. I hope you agree.

Sometimes Elva would ride the draft horse while Sundance plowed the fields. One time the plow hit a rock, causing Elva to fall off and knocking the wind out of her. She lay motionless on the ground. After freeing the plow, Sundance discovered Elva on the ground; he picked her up and revived her.

Occasionally, Sundance and Luzernia returned to Fremont to visit family. Irwin Robison's daughter Etta remembers when her younger brother Alvin Kemp was born. Sundance took Etta on his lap and told her, "she was no longer the baby and not to shed any tears." Irwin knew Butch and probably that Long was Sundance, and he knew about Etta Place, so why would he name a daughter of his Etta? That's a little strange.

Etta remembers him helping her put the saddle and bridle on a little mare for her to ride. He would call her "outlaw girl Etta" and called Alvin, "Billy the Kid." Hmm, makes you wonder, eh?

While in Fremont in 1921, they had a formal photograph taken in nearby Loa. Sundance was 60 years old and Luzernia was almost 64 in this picture, one of the four used to positively identify Bill Long as the Sundance Kid by Dr. John McCullough.

**Luzernia and the Sundance Kid
(Courtesy of Diann Forsyth Peck)**

Sundance and Luzernia grew produce and had a coup full of chickens and some turkeys and made good use of their milk cows.

They would trade their turkeys, produce, eggs, and dairy products at Hart's Market, the local store.

Even though Sundance had been a rugged cowboy, and far more than that, he would never butcher any cattle himself. He just couldn't bring himself to do the killing.

For amusement, they would read the magazine *Wild West Weekly* and laugh at the stories about the cowboys and outlaws and probably read stories about Butch Cassidy and the Sundance Kid and laugh, then laugh some more at the writer's outright attention getting fantasies. I believe as a couple grows older together, young love is replaced by something much deeper.

Later in life, Luzernia developed diabetes, and she may have had a touch of dementia as well, so Sundance attached a metal disk within reach for Luzernia to bang on when she needed help. If she banged the disc, he would hear it in the field and come running. One day, their granddaughter Elva was hitting the disk, and Bill came running. He was a little irritated when he discovered Elva did it but she never did it again.

Luzernia would give herself insulin shots, but occasionally she went into insulin shock and would become nearly unconscious. He would call Viola, who lived in Price, and she would come to Duchesne and do what she could to help. In those days so long ago, without today's wonder drugs, you wonder what pain and suffering people had to endure.

Sundance had a recurring frightening nightmare. He would shout, "There is blood on the wall! There's blood on the wall!" Luzernia would shake him and wake him up. Could this have something to do with the shootout in Cortez in 1891 where two men were killed, or the shootout near Sundance, Wyoming, where Buck Hanby was killed? Or any number of deaths he must have witnessed, or caused?

Sundance buried a "44-40 pistol" on the farm that had a brass ring attached to it. He had several guns, so why did he bury this one? Did he associate it with something bad that had happened in the past? Another mystery, this one is without any clues.

My parents frequently visited the Longs in Duchesne. My father Clayton Nickle had heard stories of Bill's extraordinary shooting ability, so he asked him for a demonstration.

My dad told me, "Bill handed me a silver dollar and said, 'Here' flip this thing in the air. I flipped it as high as I could, and you know that was the last time I ever saw that silver dollar."

After visiting his family in 1925, Butch left Circleville and went to Fremont to see Sundance. He was surprised to find that Sundance had moved away and Chloe and her husband Jerry were living there instead. Butch knew Jerry, who invited him to stay and have dinner with the family. They had a friendly cordial visit and Butch learned where Sundance lived.

After Butch left, Jerry informed Chloe that their visitor was Butch Cassidy and told her not to tell anyone of his visit.

Sundance's daughter Viola lived in Price, Utah, in 1925. Sundance and Luzernia would stay with them for the winters. After Cassidy visited his family in Circleville and my grandparents in Fremont, he went to Price to his old outlaw pal Matt Warner's saloon.

Sundance was staying with Viola when he got a message that an old friend wanted to see him. The family assumed it was an old outlaw associate but did not know which one. He left the house and did not return for several hours. When he returned, the family asked where he had been and whom he had visited. He said, "None of your business, and don't ask about it again!"

Near the end of Sundance's life, he told his grandson Silas Morrell II that in his outlaw days he had buried some gold coins in a saddlebag in a fire pit in Robbers Roost, and he suggested they go get them.

His advanced arthritis prevented him from riding a horse, so they planned to travel as far as they could in Morrell's car, and then Morrell would continue on to the gold deep in the canyon using a local's borrowed horse. He intended to use the map that Sundance had drawn which showed stones occasionally stacked as pillars along the trail as markers. The trip never happened so we will never know the exact location, but it could have been Butch Cassidy's 1896 winter camp.

In 2008, Kelly Taylor, the great grandson of George Morrell, the victim of Long's 1901 pistol whipping, discovered the trail to Butch Cassidy's 1896 and 1897 winter camp, which can only be reached by horseback. The trail has stacked rock pillars at intervals, just as the trail that Sundance described.

Taylor could not find the gold coins, but he did find some artifacts at the campsite. He found some old marbles, a mirror in a handmade metal holder, an old oil can the outlaws used to oil their pistols and some other items.

At the top of Horseshoe Canyon Taylor also discovered a tree with a very old board attached to it. Possibly, the outlaws would station a lookout near the tree after they committed a crime. If a posse were coming, the lookout would attach a flag, raise the board, and tie it up. This warning could be seen several miles below at the campsite, giving the outlaws a head start in their getaway.

Horseshoe Canyon
(Authors' Collection)

The Long household of Sundance's childhood must have been an unpleasant experience for him. There are no family stories except what we know from Viola's letter that he ran away from home. From the letter and census records we known Bill had a brother named Charles, who probably gave Sundance a picture of his sisters Sarah and Mary, as per Viola's letter. The studio name on the photograph is "J.W. Riggs, Lewiston, Idaho."

Bill Long's Sisters – Sarah and Mary Long
(Courtesy of Sherma Payton)

This picture was analyzed by Dr. McCullough along with the pictures of William Long at age 21 and the Sundance Kid picture at about

39 and determined that "it suggests a strong resemblance." It certainly should; they are his sisters.

Sundance's granddaughter Elva O'Neil said she could remember this photograph hanging on the wall in Sundance's house when she was a child. Elva remembered people referred to Mary Mahala as the M&M sister. There was a similar nickname for Sarah Salina, but she could not remember what it was.

**Sundance and Luzernia Show Off a Prized Pumpkin
(Courtesy of Diann Forsyth Peck)**

Luzernia Watches over One of Her Treasures
(Courtesy of Diann Forsyth Peck)

17
CHAPTER

The Mysterious End of Sundance

There are two completely different versions of how Sundance died. One version is from Viola's descendants; the other from Evinda's.

Viola's Version:

From 1934 to 1936, Sundance's daughter Viola lived in Salt Lake City. In the fall of 1936, Viola's husband lost his job, and they were in a desperate financial condition. Sundance could not help; he lost all the money he had when the Duchesne bank failed during the Great Depression. His response to being wiped out was, "I robbed the bank, and then the bank robbed me back."

On November 27, 1936, Viola went to Duchesne to inform Sundance and Luzernia of their financial condition and told them she could not even buy coal for the stove, let alone take them in that winter as they always had in the past. She warned they would freeze to death staying with her.

Viola Long Ehlers Salt Lake City Home Today
(Authors' Collection)

This was the first time since 1923 that Sundance and Luzernia did not stay with Viola, who helped care for them in the winter because of their physical conditions. Sundance asked Viola if she could take Luzernia in and that he would stay in Duchesne by himself. Viola said she could not even do that.

Hearing that bad news, Sundance quietly went to the bedroom, got his .22 caliber pistol, walked outside onto the front porch, and shot himself in the head. Viola never came to terms with his death. She felt responsible and grieved the rest of her life.

Suicide was a plausible conclusion. Sundance did not have any money in 1936. He was in constant pain, especially in the winters. He could no longer take care of the farm and earn his own way. He was unable to care for Luzernia and needed Viola's help.

When Dr. John McCullough, examined Sundance's skeleton in 2007, he discovered Sundance had arthritis in his back and pelvis so severe that it would have made him completely immobile at times, and the pain would have been excruciating. Dr. McCullough said he could understand why he would want to commit suicide.

Except, Dr. McCullough found that the exit wound in Sundance's skull "was not consistent with a suicide but with a murder."

Evinda's version is more in line with Dr. McCullough. Her son Roland Merkley said he found his grandfather dead with a .22 caliber rifle by his body. Evinda's husband Jerry took the rifle and threw it into the Duchesne River. They went back later and tried to retrieve it but could never find it.

Evinda was convinced that Matt Warner killed her father. It is possible that Warner wanted to identify Bill Long as Sundance in his forthcoming book and went to Duchesne to tell Sundance of his intentions. If this happened, Sundance would have demanded that Warner not identify him, and they would have gotten into an argument. It may have ended with Warner killing Sundance. Warner, who would sometimes go into violent rages, was the type of person who may have murdered Sundance.

In 1936, author Charles Kelly was doing research for his book; *Outlaw Trail a History of Butch Cassidy and His Wild Bunch*. Kelly interviewed Warner for his book, and wrote of Warner's violent tendencies and that he spent time in jail for murdering a claim jumper. Warner got a copy of Kelly's book and stayed up all night to read it. Kelly said Warner came to his office the next morning, "the angriest man I ever saw."

He told Kelly, "You are the God damn'est liar that ever lived. I'm going to sue you for libel, and if you keep selling those books, I'll burn down your establishment."

"What did I say that was wrong?" Kelly asked.

"You can call me a horse thief," Warner replied, "or a rustler or a bank robber or even a murderer, and I won't say a word. But when you say I abused my wife, you are a liar, and I'll sue you if I don't knock the hell out of you first. Where did you get such a pack of lies as you told in your book? My wife and I never had a cross word as long as she lived."

"I got it from the *Salt Lake Tribune*," Kelly said. "She told the story herself."

This took the wind out of Warner's sails.

Kelly said, "Let's get together tonight, and we will go through the book, page by page. If I made any misstatements, we can fix them up."

Warner agreed and showed up later with an apologetic smile on his face. He told Kelly he just got a call from home and had to return to Price right away.

Warner had developed kidney trouble, forcing him to quit drinking on doctor's orders. Returning to Price, he drank heavily for ten days and died on December 21, 1938. Warner's family blamed Kelly for his death.

Even though the evidence shows that Sundance was murdered, the death certificate stated his death was self-inflicted. Sundance's obituary stated his death was a suicide and that's what Kelly and Warner would have stated publically they believed.

In any event, life ended for Sundance that November 27, whatever the reason. And neither Warner nor Kelly ever identified him. The family liked Kelly, and presumably he liked them. Maybe Kelly and Warner didn't want it to be said that they drove Sundance to commit suicide by identifying him.

It's curious that Warner's book only mentions the Sundance Kid once—when stating he was killed in Bolivia—even though they knew each other for over thirty years, were outlaws together, drank together, and had many mutual friends.

Likewise, Kelly was a Butch Cassidy historian but he too never wrote anything about William Long. I suspect that like everyone else, Kelly believed the Sundance Kid was Harry Longabaugh and could not see where William Long fit in the puzzle. Both Kelly and Warner wanted to end the Butch and Sundance story with their deaths in San Vicente, Bolivia, and be done with it.

Sundance's funeral was at the Latter-Day Saints Church in Duchesne, and he was buried in the Duchesne City Cemetery. Evinda took care of Luzernia that winter, but she died the following year and was laid to rest next to her Sundance Kid.

After Long's death, his daughter Viola began the search to discover his family since she was an active Mormon and felt it was her duty to have his family genealogy recorded in the church records.

Viola searched for years, even traveling with her uncle Jack Allred, Luzernia's brother, through Idaho and as far as Canada in her search. Though she never discovered his family, her 1937 letter was the key to the discovery, which happened in 2010.   In the late 1950s, Sundance's step grandson Silas Morrell and his daughter Sherma had a copy of the same photograph that I have of Sundance. They went to Josie Bassett's small, isolated ranch near Vernal, Utah, to see if she could identify him.

Josie liked to have visitors and was friendly to them and gave them a tour of her place. Afterward, they showed her the photograph and told Josie what they knew of Sundance, including that he had two daughters with Luzernia and had lived in Duchesne, about sixty miles away.

They also told her the family knew he had been an outlaw in Butch Cassidy's gang and they hoped Josie would identify him.

When Josie saw the photograph, she said, "Oh, yes…" and then stopped! Her demeanor changed immediately and instead of being warm and welcoming she became cool and distant so they left.

They concluded that Josie did recognize the photograph but for some reason would not identify him. Perhaps Josie did not want to be in the uncomfortable position of telling them that her sister Ann was Etta Place and had gone with their grandfather to South America while he was married to their grandmother.

Josie Bassett at Her Small Ranch Near Vernal, Utah
(Internet Photo)

I hired an assistant to help me coordinate filming discoveries and events as they happened for a possible documentary. My assistant's contract included a nondisclosure agreement, which she soon ignored and proceeded to act as if she discovered the Bill Long/Sundance connection.

She contacted the *Deseret News* in Salt Lake City without my authorization and told them that we were going to exhume William Long's remains. Even though I was disappointed at the time the publicity that followed was critical in completing the research. The exhumation created quite a stir. Reporter Geoff Liesik was there and wrote this article that was published in the December 16, 2008 issue.

Is Sundance Really Buried In Duchesne
By Geoff Liesik Deseret News
Published Tuesday, Dec. 16, 2008

DUCHESNE — The bones of a man buried in the city cemetery 72 years ago have been exhumed for testing to determine whether he is actually Harry Alonzo Longabaugh, better known to most of the world as the Sundance Kid.

The skeletal remains of William Henry Long were disinterred Friday by a University of Utah anthropologist and the executive director of a Salt Lake City genetics lab as some of Long's relatives looked on. A documentary film crew recorded the event.

Long took his own life at his home outside Duchesne on Nov. 27, 1936, according to his step-granddaughter Etta Forsyth. Forsyth, 91, still refers to Long as her "Uncle Billy." She remembers him as kind and loving toward her grandmother, who had six children when she married Long in 1895 after her first husband was killed in a logging accident.

"My mom just knew he was part of the outlaw gang but didn't ever know who he really was," said Forsyth's daughter Diane Peck, who was with her mother at Friday's exhumation.

University of Utah biological anthropologist John M. McCullough, in an affidavit used to obtain a court order to exhume the remains said he compared a known photograph of Long against a known photograph of Longabaugh/Sundance.

"It is clear that these two photographs are of the same person," McCullough told the court.

In a telephone interview with the Uintah Basin Standard, Dr. McCullough said he was able to take linear measurements from the two photos and found them to be "almost too good."

"I'd compare the ratios in one photo to the other and it was almost a line," he said. "This was just absolutely beyond belief. It was just so close."

Provo attorney Thomas Seiler represents five of the seven Long descendants who sought to have the remains tested. He said his clients want to determine their ancestor's true identity so they can complete genealogy work as part of their Mormon faith.

"They keep hitting a wall with him," Seiler told the Standard. They can't find anyone behind him."

Speculation that Long and Longabaugh — sometimes misspelled Longabaugh — is the same person has grown stronger in recent years."

Long's skull and a femur were dug up several years ago by another relative, according to family members involved in the most recent exhumation. The individual had a rectangular piece of bone cut from the femur, apparently to conduct DNA tests. The results of those tests are unknown.

In November 2007, Long's remains — including the skull and femur — were reburied in the original grave site. The bones were placed in a vault.

"We were trying to reverse the '"ethical damage,'" McCullough said.

According to Long's headstone, he was born in February 1860. His obituary in the Dec. 4th 1936 edition of the Uintah Basin Record identifies him as a Duchesne farmer, born and raised in Wyoming's Big Horn Basin. It doesn't provide the name of a specific town in Wyoming, though.

Longabaugh was born in Pennsylvania in early 1867, according to the historical record, and moved to Colorado at 15 to homestead with a cousin. He earned his outlaw moniker after serving time in Sundance, Wyo., for stealing a horse and saddle in 1887.

The Sundance Kid's association with Utah native Robert Leroy Parker, aka Butch Cassidy and the Wild Bunch is believed to have begun nine years later in 1896.

A loose confederation of criminals, the Wild Bunch was credited with numerous bank and train robberies throughout the Midwest and

West. Some, including Sundance, used an area of the Big Horn Basin known as the Hole-in-the-Wall to hide out from posses after their heists.

John Barton, a senior lecturer in history at Utah State University, said Sundance would have had a healthy geographical knowledge of the Uintah Basin during his time on the outlaw trail. Local history has members of the Wild Bunch frequenting Nine Mile Canyon and the homesteads of John Jarvie and Herb Bassett in Brown's Park near the Colorado-Utah-Wyoming border.

"They were well acquainted here," said Barton, who teaches at Utah State's Uintah Basin campus and is not involved in McCullough's inquiry into a possible link between Longabaugh and Long.

"Those guys would have known all the routes," Barton said. "I have personally talked to people who knew them or knew people who knew them, but that's folklore."

Historians say Butch and Sundance left the country in 1901 for South America with Sundance's common-law wife, Etta Place. Place, whose true identity also remains in dispute, later returned to the United States. It's unclear if or when the two men returned to the country permanently.

In 1908, when a courier for a Bolivian silver mine was robbed of the company payroll, he fingered two Americans. The bandits — believed by some to be Butch and Sundance — were cornered inside a rooming house by authorities and killed in an ensuing gun battle.

They were buried together in an unmarked grave that remains undiscovered, leaving doubt about whether the two dead men were in fact the infamous American outlaws. Several individuals have come forward over the years claiming they were Butch or Sundance, or that they spoke to the men after 1908. So far, historians have disputed each claim.

In her 1975 book, Cassidy's sister, Lula Parker Betenson, said her brother visited her following the Bolivian shootout and said he and Sundance were not involved. She said her brother died in the Pacific Northwest in 1937 under the alias William Phillips.

"I have never believed they were killed in South America," Barton said, adding that McCullough's findings are "really kind of exciting."

"This is prima facie evidence," he said. "It's not, 'Grandma knew somebody who ran into Butch.'"

Still, for Barton, confirmation that Longabaugh and Long are one and the same would be bittersweet, given the romanticism that surrounds the legends of Butch and Sundance.

"As the mystery is solved and (Sundance) lives out his life as a poor farmer, probably struggling to make ends meet, raising a whole brood of not-his-own children, that's not as exciting as our imagination might run," Barton said. "It takes that element of the wild and exciting out of it."

The remains collected from Long's grave Friday will undergo a more refined analysis by McCullough sometime this week. Then DNA samples will be collected at Sorenson Genomics in Salt Lake City. They'll be tested against known samples from Longabaugh's family.

McCullough said it could take up to three months before results are available, depending on the quality of the DNA recovered.

"Only on TV do you get results in minutes," he said.

With the publication of this article interest in the subject was huge. The comments made by readers following the article numbered in the hundreds. The *Deseret News* decided to publish a follow up article that included an interview with Long's granddaughter Etta Forsyth.

Was Duchesne farmer the Sundance Kid?
By Geoff Liesik, Deseret News
Published: Tuesday, Feb. 17, 2009, 12:00 a.m. MST

DUCHESNE — Is a farmer who died here in 1936 actually one of the Old West's most legendary outlaws?

Etta Forsyth isn't so sure.

Forsyth is the step-granddaughter of William Henry Long, the man whose remains were exhumed from the Duchesne City Cemetery in December for forensic testing to determine whether he is really Harry Alonzo Longabaugh, alias the Sundance Kid.

Forsyth, 91, still refers to Long as her "Uncle Billy."

"When Grandma married Bill Long, all the kids by Silas Morrell were older and I think they called him Uncle Billy," Forsyth said. "So we all called him Uncle Billy."

Long married Morrell's widow, Luzernia, in November 1894. She was 36 and had six children from her first marriage, including Forsyth's mother Clara. Long listed his age as 27 on the marriage license filed in Wayne County, which is seven years younger than he, should have been, according to the birth date listed on his headstone. The Sundance Kid was 27 years old in 1894.

Clara Morrell would later marry I. G. Robison and give birth to Forsyth and five other children. Forsyth said Long worked for her father on his ranch near the Henry Mountains in central Utah earning $2 a day.

"He'd sit you on his knee and hum to you," Forsyth said. "I can't see how he was a mean man. He was an outlaw, we knew that right from the first, but I don't think he was Sundance."

Long was a good cook who kept a clean house and doted on his wife, according to Forsyth, who was 19 when he died. He was also an accomplished marksman, able to shoot the heads off nails on the family garage with a pistol. It was a pastime he engaged in with his son-in-law, Robison, who served as Wayne County sheriff from 1913 to 1915.

Forsyth said she never heard Long talk about his past. "If he did, he talked about it to my dad," she said. "Dad couldn't say anything, he was the sheriff."

Still Long did, on at least one occasion, display a propensity for violence. The Oct. 24, 1901, Deseret News reported that Long had pistol-whipped a relative in a dispute over irrigation water. The gun had discharged during the incident, grazing the man's head.

"Uncle George was a water thief," Forsyth said when asked about the incident. "He lived right by the canal and he got (the water) first."

Long, fearing that he'd mortally wounded the man, fled Fremont and vowed never to return if the man died. When he survived, Long returned home. Forsyth said her grandparents later moved to Duchesne at the urging of their daughter, Evinda, who had married a man from the Uintah Basin. She said her father told her Long was gone for two weeks and came back with the money to pay off the land for the family's new ranch.

"He had something hid up to Fish Lake," said Forsyth, who taught in the Granite School District for 20 years.

"Butch Cassidy's nephew was one of my students," she said. "He told me Butch died on his mother's porch, not in South America."

Dianne Peck, Forsyth's daughter, said she's found census records that list Luzernia Long as the head of household during the years that Butch and Sundance were living in South America.

There are also at least two instances of Luzernia Long purchasing property in her husband's name during the same time.

"I think he and Butch figured on going to Bolivia and making some money," Peck said, "and I think they did."

Historians say Butch and Sundance left the U.S. in 1901 for South America with Sundance's common-law wife, Etta Place. That couple's union would have occurred after Long had married Luzernia, something that doesn't surprise Forsyth.

"I think he was still kind of an outlaw when he went and married (Place)," she said, seeming to concede, at least for a moment, that Long and Sundance may have been the same man.

Place, whose true identity also remains in dispute, later returned to the United States. No one's been able to prove definitively, though, whether Butch or Sundance ever returned to the country permanently. Many believe Butch and Sundance were killed in a 1908 shootout with Bolivian authorities following a payroll robbery. The slain men were buried together in an unmarked grave that remains undiscovered, leaving doubt about whether they were in fact the infamous American outlaws.

Peck said her grandfather told her about meeting Cassidy after he was rumored to have died in South America. She said the outlaw was sick when he showed up on the former sheriff's doorstep. After being nursed back to health, Cassidy offered Robison his rifle out of gratitude, Peck said. Her grandfather initially refused the gun, but ultimately accepted it.

"He said, 'Butch told me he never shot a man, but don't turn your back on Sundance,'" Peck recalled with a laugh. Still, Forsyth maintains that Long was "tenderhearted." He had to hire out the slaughtering of livestock, she said, and therefore is an unlikely candidate for the role of blood-thirsty outlaw. But her son-in-law, Jerry Peck, believes anything's possible.

"I don't think whether he was a gentleman or not is really a criterion because some real gentlemen aren't always that gentle," Jerry Peck said.

In fact, family members said they're now unsure whether Long's death was actually a suicide, the official cause listed on his death certificate. Forsyth said one of Long's grandsons found him lying next to a .22-caliber rifle on Nov. 27, 1936, and everyone assumed Long had taken his own life.

"But it could have been someone who caught up to him from the past," she said.

Jerry Nickle has always suspected his great-grandfather was the Sundance Kid."

Four samples have been collected from Long's remains by Sorenson Forensics in Salt Lake City. The samples have been sent to an undisclosed lab for testing against known DNA from the Longabaugh family. Results are expected in four to eight weeks.

The skeletal remains have also been examined by biological anthropologist John M. McCullough. The University of Utah professor's comparison of photos of Longabaugh and Long helped secure a court order to exhume Long for further study.

McCullough's analysis revealed identical traits in both men, including a notch in an ear, evidence of a broken nose and a cleft chin. There are also matches in height, hair color, and eye color. It was noted that in the famous "Fort Worth Five" photo of the Wild Bunch, the Sundance Kid's fingers on his right hand are curled under. Long's fingers on his right hand are also curled under in the same manner in a later photograph taken with Luzernia.

Asked again how certain she is that her step-grandfather isn't Sundance, Forsyth answered: "I sure feel like I'm sure, but I'd be glad to see it solved."

Interest in these articles prompted KSL television from Salt Lake City to air two reports during this time, with one of them going national on MSNBC.

By the time the last report was broadcast, we had completed the Harry Longabaugh DNA comparison. It was conclusive that the William Long DNA did not match the Harry Longabaugh DNA as we had hoped.

I could not understand why the DNA did not match. I was convinced by my research that Long was the Sundance Kid.

The last *Deseret News* article was published December 28, 2009:

Digging up the past: Man sure relative was 'Sundance Kid'
By Geoff Liesik, Deseret News
Published: Monday, Dec. 28, 2009, 12:00 a.m. MST

DUCHESNE — Questions about the true identity of a man who died in November 1936 are still unanswered more than a year after his remains were exhumed from the Duchesne City Cemetery.

Was William Henry Long simply a destitute farmer with an enigmatic past and a bleak future?

Or was he actually Harry Alonzo Longabaugh — the man history knows better as the Sundance Kid, living under an assumed name in a small northeastern Utah town, years after his reported death in South America?

Jerry Nickle began his quest more than six years ago to flesh out his step-great-grandfather's real past. That search led to an exhumation of Long's remains on Dec. 12, 2008, by the executive director of Salt Lake City-based Sorenson Forensics.

A subsequent comparison of the genetic material extracted from Long's badly decayed skeleton and a sequence of DNA from known descendants of the Longabaugh family yielded an inconclusive result with regard to a familial relationship.

"I was disappointed because I know dang well it's him," Nickle told the Deseret News from his home in Gilbert, Ariz. "I was just puzzled," he said. "As a kid I heard the stories about him riding with Butch Cassidy, that he robbed trains and banks. It was so fascinating to me."

Nickle said the presence of underground water in the cemetery where Long was interred, and the resulting disintegration of his wooden casket, makes it possible that his bones have been contaminated. There was an earlier exhumation by another relative, in September 2006 which Nickle termed "unauthorized," that raises additional concerns about contamination.

He speculated there's also the possibility that there may not be a genetic link between Long and the Longabaugh family because of "hanky-panky" somewhere in the past or possibly an adoption.

"You're never exactly sure because you never know what happened back there, like something that broke that genetic line someplace," said Nickle, who is working on a book and screenplay about the project.

Nickle plans to have Long's remains sent to another lab for additional DNA analysis. But no matter what the genetic tests reveal, Nickle believes the circumstantial evidence linking Long and Longabaugh is overwhelming.

According to Long's headstone, he was born in February 1860. His obituary says he was reared in Wyoming's Bighorn Basin, near the Hole-in-the-Wall hideout later used by outlaws but doesn't name a specific town. Nickle said no one has been able to locate Long's birth certificate.

Longabaugh was born in Pennsylvania in early 1867, according to the historical record, and moved to Colorado at 15 to homestead with a cousin. He earned his outlaw moniker after serving time in Sundance, Wyo., for stealing a horse and saddle in 1887. His association with Utah native Robert Leroy Parker — aka Butch Cassidy — and the Wild Bunch is believed to have begun nine years later in 1896.

Long had married Nickle's great-grandmother, Luzernia Morrell, two years earlier. The pair met while her first husband was still alive but suffering from serious injuries that would later kill him.

Nickle said Long rode into the Morrell's camp after he was wounded in a gunfight in Cortez, Colo. Luzernia Morrell tended the wound, and Long followed the family back to Wayne County, Utah.

When Long and Morrell wed in 1894, she was 36 and had six children from her first marriage. Long listed his age as 27 on the marriage license. That was seven years younger than he should have been according to the birth date listed on his headstone, but identical to Longabaugh's age in 1894.

Besides the family history, Nickle points to striking similarities found in authenticated photographs of Long and Longabaugh as evidence that the men are one and the same. Photo similarities: Their belief is bolstered by the work of University of Utah anthropology professor John M. McCullough, another person involved in the 2008 exhumation. McCullough studied the similarities in the Long/Longabaugh photos. In court papers filed to obtain permission to exhume Long, the anthropologist declared: "It is clear that these two photographs are of the (same) person."

McCullough's photo analysis revealed identical traits in both men — including a notch in an ear, evidence of a broken nose, and a cleft chin. There are also matches in height, hair color, and eye color.

Once Long's remains were unearthed, McCullough conducted a physical examination of the bones as well. That analysis revealed that Long may not have committed suicide, as his death certificate stated. McCullough found evidence that the .22-caliber bullet that killed Long entered his skull from an angle that indicates someone else shot him.

Two stories of Sundance's death: Nickle knows two family stories about how Long died. As one daughter told it, the Great Depression left her parents bankrupt. The woman said when she told Long she wouldn't be able to host her parents in her Wasatch Front home during the winter of 1936, he left his home and shot himself in the head.

"It was said that he robbed banks and then the bank robbed him," Nickle said. "I don't know how much money he had, but they were in desperate financial straits by 1936."

Long's other daughter said her father got into an argument with Matt Warner, a former Wild Bunch associate who left the outlaw trail and later became a Carbon County lawman. One possible reason for the dispute was Warner's plan to publish a book about his days on the wrong side of the law. The fight escalated and Warner killed Long, according to the family story.

"How do you explain two different versions? I don't have an explanation for it," said Nickle, who is unsure which account to believe.

What he does believe though is that a collection of documents he refers to as "The Pinkerton Files" offers solid evidence that Long was really Longabaugh. The handwritten or typed reports were compiled by agents with the Pinkerton National Detective Agency. One of the reports, a copy of which Nickle provided to the Deseret News, indicates that Longabaugh visited a hospital in Buffalo, N.Y., in 1901, where he was treated for a bullet wound to the leg suffered "in the Far West." Nickle maintains that the injury is identical to the one Long sustained during the Cortez shootout.

Nickle also points to a Pinkerton report that Longabaugh suffered from a chronic sinus problem. He believes the malady was the result of a severely broken nose sustained during the outlaw's legitimate time as a cowboy breaking horses. He said Long also had difficulty breathing through his nose.

"The Pinkerton Files are the best evidence for me," Nickle said. They confirm everything."

But Dan Buck, a critic of the effort to link Long and Longabaugh, isn't so sure. "I don't know specifically what Jerry Nickle is referring to in terms of Pinkerton information," Buck said. "I've never encountered a single document that indicates William Henry Long is the Sundance Kid."

Buck has researched and written about the history of Butch and Sundance with his wife, Anne Meadows, since 1986. Based in Washington, D.C., the couple has traveled to South America and visited the places where the outlaws lived and worked in the early 1900s.

"There's always room for debate about any historical controversy," said Buck, who was part of an unsuccessful effort in 1991 with Meadows and noted forensic anthropologist Clyde Snow to identify the remains of two men buried in Bolivia as Butch and Sundance.

Buck said he and Meadows, over the years, have identified 60 different versions of how Butch and Sundance died. In those stories the outlaws supposedly died in North America, South America, or Europe.

"That gives you a sense of how much is out there in terms of folklore, personal stories, family stories, newspaper accounts and so on," Buck said. "History hates a vacuum."

Buck said Butch and Sundance "really did disappear" at the time of their deaths, which promoted the myth that the men survived the 1908 Bolivian gun battle where Buck and Meadows believe they lost their lives. Long, he said, is simply one more "pretender" being offered up in another of the "resurrection stories" that inevitably surround outlaws.

"There's a whole area of outlaw folklore about the disappearance and the return of the bandit; the return of the bandit representing hope for the community," Buck said. "I think Jerry Nickle has fallen into this because he's so determined to prove (Long is Longabaugh) that he will find any scrap of paper to prove it and not look at the entire picture."

Buck described the Pinkerton files in general as "functioning sort of like flypaper for facts, rumors, stories, informant accounts, and letters from people who saw something in the newspaper. Everything is in the files and you have to go through everything and try to piece together, if you can, an account of what really happened."

Nickle said he understands the skepticism surrounding his claims about Long and Longabaugh. He said he doubted a connection early in his own research; that he searched for evidence to disprove a link *as much as to prove one. But, he said, those critical of his findings are motivated by a jealous desire to have their own work recognized as the definitive answer to the question: What really happened to the Sundance Kid?*

"Just wait until all my compiled research is presented in book form and then tell me where I'm wrong. You just can't deny it," Nickle said. "What is coming will knock people's socks off."

These articles received nearly two thousand online comments, including many by some of the best informed Cassidy and Sundance researchers. None of these people completely agree on everything that Cassidy and Sundance did and probably never will. But these experts challenged me and helped me.

In the comment section that followed one of the articles a reader had discovered and identified the census record where Sundance was enumerated with his parents and siblings. This was the final major piece of the puzzle I was looking for.

The similarities of the Bill Long, Sundance Kid photographs that had first sparked my interest were conclusive; Bill Long was the Sundance Kid. And with more research it all became clear why the Sundance DNA did not match the Longabaugh DNA. I had it half right. It wasn't Longabaugh using William Long as an alias; William Long had used Longabaugh as *his* alias. It was a twist that almost eluded everyone.

Apparently, I inherited a bit of Butch and Sundance's luck to make the final connection.

The story of William Henry Long, aka the Sundance Kid, is so captivating that I knew I had to share it with everyone, along with the efforts and revelations that surrounded my search and discoveries.

Morrell Sisters with half Sister Viola Long
Chloe Clara Mary Martha Viola
(Courtesy of Diann Forsyth Peck)

18
CHAPTER

Proof William Long Was the Sundance Kid

Wshed**W**illiam Long's family had never been able to confirm his genealogy or birthplace so his descendants petitioned the court to exhume Long's remains to conduct a DNA comparison to see if his family ancestry could be established. The court approved his exhumation.

Sorenson Genomics of Salt Lake City performed a DNA test and Tim Kupherschmid of Sorenson put me in contact with Dr. John McCullough.

We filmed the exhumation and Dr. McCullough's and Kupherschmid initial examination at the grave site.

Dr. McCullough and Tim Kupherschmid, Meet the Sundance Kid
(Courtesy of Michael Karr)

We also filmed Dr. McCullough as he did a more detailed forensic examination and photograph comparison analysis at his laboratory at the University of Utah.

Upon completion, Dr. McCullough issued his report, which concluded that William "Sundance" Long died of a gunshot wound to the head. A scientific analysis showed that his hips and lower back were damaged by the years he spent breaking horses.

Confirmed: Historical records state that Sundance was a bronco-buster. Dr. McCullough's report also presented a scientific analysis of a bullet wound to the leg that Long suffered in Cortez in 1891, just before he met Luzernia.

Confirmed: The leg wound found in Dr. McCullough's exhumation report directly correlates to the Pinkerton report that states Sundance received a gunshot wound in the west, adding another crucial piece of the puzzle.

Dr. McCullough added "this individual would be approximately 5'8" tall at death but slightly taller when alive. The Sundance Kid was reported to be 5'9" in stature.

Dr. McCullough also did a computerized comparison of the Sundance Kid in the Fort Worth Five photographs and my family photograph of William Long when he was 21.

Transparency Overlay
(Courtesy of Dr. John McCullough)

This is the transparency overlay used by Dr. McCullough. The top transparency is of William Long at age 21. Below is Sundance in the FW 5 picture, age 39. As you can see, the facial features blend together without any deviation. You can see the shadow of the distinctive round top hat that Sundance wore in the Fort Worth Five photo and Long's cowboy hat on the top transparency.

Dr. McCullough concluded "It is absolutely clear that the photo of Mr. William Long taken in 1892 and the assumed picture of Mr. Longabaugh taken with the wild bunch are of the same person."

William H. Long   Sundance Kid

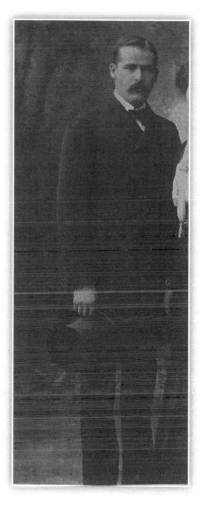

Older William H. Long   **Sundance Kid**

All these men are in fact the same man: William H. Long, the real Sundance Kid. And he did not commit suicide; he was *murdered*!

Remember, we first surmised that the Sundance Kid was Harry Longabaugh and he was using the alias William Long. Now we know it was the other way around: William Long used the name Harry Longabaugh as an alias.

So, initially we were only half right. Longabaugh was the name everyone in the Old West thought the Sundance Kid's real name was, but now we know the real facts.

The photo analysis and Dr. McCullough's other conclusions taken together with all the coincidences, the family information, the Pinkerton files, and the circumstantial evidence I've presented throughout this book prove beyond a reasonable doubt that William H. Long, not Harry Longabaugh, and was the one and only Sundance Kid.

19
CHAPTER

The Reburial Of Sundance

After the forensic examination and the DNA tests were completed, the remains of Sundance were reburied on September 23, 2010, in the Duchesne City Cemetery.

At least fifty family members attended the ceremony. The original pine box that Sundance was buried in had deteriorated, so a new wooden casket, a replica of the period, was used and placed into a new concrete vault.

The wooden lid was laid on the casket and each family member hammered a square nail into the lid, fastening it to the casket. I had the honor of driving in the first nail, which was over 100 years old. It was a very emotional moment for me personally.

Me Driving the First Nail
(Authors' Collection)

A few toddlers, the fifth generation of Sundance's descendents, were there and with a little help, they each drove a nail as well.

A horse drawn hearse carried the casket the final one hundred yards. Except, instead of horses, family members wearing cowboy hats pulled the hearse by hand the final yards.

Family and Friends Pull the Hearse to the Grave Site
(Authors' Collection)

At the grave site, professional country and western singer Mary Kay played an acoustic guitar and sang "Amazing Grace" and other gospel songs. She was dressed in the finest cowgirl attire.

Mary Kay Sings At The Grave Site
(Authors' Collection)

Local Mormon Bishop and family member Jerry Peck said a prayer and then the casket was lowered into the vault, and the vault lid was lowered into place. Each person there put a shovel of dirt onto the vault, and then it was over.

Deseret News reporter Geoff Liesik was there to gather information for an article. The event was filmed for future use, hopefully a documentary.

**A Little Lighthearted Fun: Mary Kay and Kelly Taylor
(Authors' Collection)**

I have been consumed with the story of William Long and those he associated with since before 2004. The more I discovered, the more questions I had. I hope with the publication of this book, some interested reader or unknown relative will come forward and contact me at jnickle364@yahoo.com with information about, or answers to, some of the mysteries that still need to be solved.

What happened to Butch Cassidy? Where did he go and did he have a family or children? Are there any descendents? What happened to the real Harry Longabaugh? Did he die an old man in Canada? Did he have a family with descendants who live today?

What happened to Nora/Etta? Did she have a son at the Denver hospital? Are there relatives who are her descendants yet to be discovered? What about Sundance's brothers and sisters, the James Long descendants? They certainly can be found with research. They probably do not know that their relative was the Sundance Kid. What will their reactions be when they find out? Do they have stories, too?

20
CHAPTER

Who Killed The Sundance Kid?

We all die, some more peacefully than others and that was true for Sundance and those he loved best.

Luzernia Allred (Morrell) Long

On March 11, 1937, the wife and confidant of the Sundance Kid for over 45 years left this earth for her place in God's house. She died at 78 years-old in her Duchesne, Utah, home. Her eight children and many more grandchildren surrounded her.

She was one of a few ruggedly strong, founding pioneers of Wayne County, Utah; she was a loving mother, grandmother, great-grand-mother, great-great-grandmother, and now great-great-great-grand-mother who bound her family closely together.

She lies at rest in the Duchesne Cemetery next to her beloved Sundance. Her descendants live among you today and carry with them her enduring love for family. That's just the way she would want it.

My children and I have the honor of being among her direct descendants. We pass things along to our children; is there any reason that our great grandparents didn't pass knowledge on to our grandparents and them to our parents, and them to us? All this wonderful knowledge was possible because of a gunfight in Cortez, Colorado, in 1891·

Salute, great grandmother.

Robert Leroy Parker (Butch Cassidy)

According to his sister, Lula Parker Bentenson, only their family knows the date of his death and where Butch was laid to rest, but some believe that he passed away in New Mexico at the age of 70. Others believe he died in Nevada or in Washington State and put his demise in 1937.

Ms. Bentenson claims her father said, "Leroy was chased all his life; let's leave him in peace." He didn't want Butch's "grave site vandalized."

I think it's okay to say that I love Butch Cassidy too and I hope he didn't suffer in his last years like Sundance. Without Butch, there probably would not have been a Sundance, and vice versa. I think Butch's father was right: leave him in peace.

William Henry Long (The Sundance Kid)

An unknown assailant shot Sundance in the head on November 27, 1936. By all accounts of the many who knew him firsthand, he loved his family more than anything else. In his later years he developed a good sense of humor and perhaps he had it all along with his children and grandchildren.

I suppose that when he was younger, his childhood may have been the cause for his mostly somber disposition along with his being tossed into jail for someone else. He was one of the West's most endearing bandits and, like Butch; he gave to others in need just like Robin Hood.

As for me, despite some of his negative actions, I love him as a son loves his father, and I wish I could have known him.

So who was it that killed the Sundance Kid? That's a question I would love to have the definitive answer to! Perhaps, to get it, it's back to the drawing board for me.

According to his daughter Evinda, Sundance was shot in the head near his corral with a rifle lying near where he fell. Dr. John M.

McCullough examined Sundance's exhumed remains and confirmed it could not have been a self-inflicted wound, invalidating Viola's claim it was suicide. I cannot know for sure why she made up the story. Maybe she didn't want anyone to think his nefarious deeds had led to murder. Or perhaps she was in denial that anyone could kill her daddy, a infamous gunslinger.

Evinda believed it was Matt Warner but many others may have also wanted revenge once they found out who he really was and where he lived.

Maybe it was a mercy killing. A senior citizen of 75 in 1936, Sundance suffered excruciating hip and back pain with no relief given the limited medication available so perhaps a trusted friend ended his misery. If that was the case, it could only be his true friend of over 50 years, Butch Cassidy.

Whoever shot him, I sincerely hope that as the bullet entered, his pain vanished and Sundance was whisked off at light speed to God's loving care.

The next time you see a man sitting on a range horse with an old saddle and wearing worn boots, chaps, a hat, and a rugged, unshaven face, you will be seeing one of a dying breed of real cowboys tending to his business. I've admired what they do all my life.

May God bless them all, including my great grandpa, the Sundance Kid.

Epilogue

In 2007 I entered into an agreement with a professional to film the discoveries of my ongoing research and the ensuing events as they transpired. Hopefully these many hours of footage will be used for a documentary.

We interviewed and filmed Etta Forsyth and Elva O'Neil, the last two people alive who actually knew Sundance. We also filmed many old timers who knew part of the story.

We toured and filmed the magnificent scenery on the very trails that Cassidy and Sundance used around Wayne County and the Robbers Roost, with friends and relatives riding horses like true cowboys and cowgirls.

We used the old train at Heber City and staged a holdup of the train and a bank robbery in the old town. There were ten cowboys and as many character actors that played parts as the bank was robbed and the train held up. The character actors played frightened train passengers and town citizens. Some cowboys played the robbers and others played the sheriff and posse.

Heber City is surrounded by the magnificent Rocky Mountains that can be seen in the background. The modern ski resort of Sundance is located five miles to the west. Robert Redford established this resort in 1969 and named it as homage to his character in *Butch Cassidy and the Sundance Kid.*

Duchesne, the town where the real Sundance Kid lived and died, is located about 85 miles to the east. All of these locations are within roughly a 50 mile radius.

Cast and film Crew Preparing to Rob the Train.
(Courtesy of Christine Karr)

Robbers Chasing Train
(Courtesy of Christine Karr)

Robbing The Train
(Courtesy of Christine Karr)

ROBERS COMING TO TOWN
(Courtesy of Christine Karr)

Bank Robbers
(Courtesy of Christine Karr)

I also contracted with a writer for a screenplay prior to the publication of this book. The script has been completed for quite a while, so we are ready for Hollywood. With Butch and Sundance's luck, we will see Butch Cassidy and the Sundance Kid on the big screen again.

Jerry Nickle Wanted Poster
(Sketch by Kami Taylor)

That scoundrel C.J. put this wanted poster of me here without my knowledge. He said it's only fitting 'cause banditry runs deep in my ancestry. I guess I can't argue with that! But, I'd still like to meet C.J. out by the corral. Not with pistols like Sundance but I think I can take him in a quick draw face-slapping contest!

On July 10, 2013 my coauthor, C. J. Del Barto and myself presented an autographed copy of this book to Wyoming's Governor Mead. We rode to the capitol steps in Cheyenne by horseback to give the book to the Governor. The media was there and covered the event. Here is the link to the "Bringing Sundance Home" Facebook, where the video can be seen. www.facebook.com/BringingSundanceHome.

There are other videos that can also be seen on the Facebook page. For the latest developments you can follow us on Facebook.

Here is the Website: http://bringingsundancehome.com.

You can email me directly at: jnickle364@yahoo.com.

Appendix A: Dr. McCullough's Report

PRELIMINARY REPORT

EXAMINATION OF WILLIAM HENRY LONG OF DUCHESNE, UTAH

15 November 2007

In mid-October I received a telephone call   concerning the possibility of a forensic examination of an interred decedent who may have been buried under a pseudonym. The decedent, Mr. William Henry Long, died in 1936 and was interred in the city cemetery, Duchesne, Utah.   suggested that Mr. Long might have been born a Mr. Henry Longabaugh, of Montvate, Pennsylvania, better known in the western United States as the Sundance Kid, a wanted criminal originally thought to have died in South America.

On 26 October 2007 I attended the disinterment of Mr. Long. Already exhumed had been major portion of his skull, a portion of the hyoid bone, a calcified section of the larynx, a humerus and a femur, a large section of which had been sectioned for DNA analysis by Sorensen Genomics. After exhumation of all recoverable parts the skeleton was laid out in anatomical order to discern any osteological lesions or anomalies.

The skull had been significantly damaged by an apparent self-inflicted 22-calibre GSW to the left temple about 3 centimeters superior and 2 cm posterior to the external auditory meatus. The inferior portion of the temporal bone was shattered and dislocated from the upper portion. The rebound effect of the blast was to disassociate the lower half of the face and skull base from the remainder of the skull. In field circumstances facial reconstruction was impossible. An additional complication was the edentulous state of the decedent, with complete and apparently simultaneous tooth loss only some 2 to 5 years before death, as the alveolar borders had completely healed, but not significantly retreated from their earlier positions. Rapid examination of the skull revealed classic Caucasian features a sharp nasal spine, a sharp inferior nasal border, and a small, narrow palatal surface.

Examination of the postcranial skeleton revealed significant arthritic development along the borders of the lumbar centra 3-5 and to a lesser degree, thoracic 10-12 and lumbar 1-3; accompanying this were arthritic outgrowths along the superior and lateral borders of the sacrum. The fifth lumbar vertebra also showed signs of fracture of the posterior portion of the vertebra, a condition known as spondylolysis; this is caused by a series of micro-fractures from frequent pressure on the vertebra by activities such as heavy athletic activity. The result would be very painful. The acetabula and femoral heads were also deeply involved in arthritic growths along the articular surfaces, probably making walking very painful directly in the hip, but also along the lower spine and possibly legs with restriction of nerves from the vertebral arthritis.

An exostosis on the anterior medial surface of the proximal end of the tibia was noted. A radiograph was obtained and examined by a local doctor who stated that the origin of the exostosis was unclear. A metal detector was applied to the surface with a completely negative reading; the radiograph likewise showed an absence of dense material consistent with the presence of metal.

As a general observation, the long bones had exceptionally well-developed ridging along the muscle lines, indicating that the individual had highly developed musculature and undoubtedly lead a very active life. Stature was estimated from all long bones but the right fibula which had broken with non-matching ends, making measurement impossible. Results are found in Appendix A. The stature suggested for this individual would be approximately 5' 8" tall. The Sundance Kid was reported to be either 5' 10" or 5' 9" in stature. Our estimate is quite close to these early reports if one considers the general inaccuracy of casual observations, and the use of high-heeled Western boots by many in the region.

Photo examination was carried out on the following pictures:

Longabaugh with the "Wild Bunch"
Longabaugh with Etta Place in New York
William Long in 1892
William Long in old age with his wife
McCarty, Pere
McCarty, Fille
Longabaugh Sisters in Pennsylvania
Two women found in a photo purportedly taken in Idaho.

Measurement were made of the individuals along the facial midline, as the faces in different photographs were posed at different angles, making accurate lateral measurements impossible. Because the faces are at unknown scales, ratios of various facial measurements were the only fair means of comparison. The ratios represent facial proportions. Results of the examination are found in Appendix B as charts. Each chart is a one-on-one comparison of two individuals; a straight line indicates identity while dots which deviate from a straight line indicate differences in the facial proportions; the greater the deviation the less likely the individuals portrayed are identical. The photos were generally dark and unclear, making measurements extremely difficult. In future, the application of photo enhancement techniques would make the photos much easier to read.

It is absolutely clear that the photo of Mr. William Long taken in 1892 and the photo of Mr. Harry Longabaugh taken with the "Wild Bunch" are of the same person. Comparison of photos of Mr. Long in 1892 and with his wife many years later yield very different results. I believe that the results are changed because of tooth loss in the latter photo that dramatically alters Mr. Long's facial proportions. The pictures of Mr. Long are not consistent with the photos of either of the McCartys.

It is slightly less clear that the women in both photos are his sisters, although the lines of concordance are very strong. Certainly it is not unreasonable to think that the woman standing in one photo is the woman sitting in the other (A1 to A2 and B1 to B2). As with most of the other photos, photo enhancement techniques would yield more accurate results.

A last type of inspection was visual. Transparencies were prepared for comparing faces posed at similar (but unfortunately not identical) angles. These are placed at the end of the report as Appendix C. It will be immediately apparent that the photo of Mr. Long in 1892 and Mr. Longabaugh as one of the "Wild Bunch" are two photos of the same person. Although the pose angles are somewhat different, the points of similarity along the nose, the Mitchell's Notch on the chin and the peculiar shape of the ear pinnae are all absolutely identical. Comparing the late photo of Mr. Long and the New York photo of Mr. Longabaugh with Etta Place is less successful, in part because these photos were taken many years apart, the faces are oriented differently along the horizontal plane, and, I suspect, after Mr. Long had his teeth removed.

Comparison of the two sisters with the women Mr. Long claimed to be sisters is difficult because of the different angles for the two women in the two photos. Nonetheless, comparison of the women on the midline – the one sitting in one photo with the woman standing in the other – suggests a strong resemblance. As in other photos, I suspect the photos were taken many years apart so some amount of aging will have occurred, including possible tooth loss.

Conclusion.

It seems clear that all evidence – osteological, anthropometric and visual - is consistent with the hypothesis that Mr. William Henry Long of Duchesne, Utah, was a pseudonym for Mr. Harry Longabaugh, also known as the Sundance Kid. Photo of the Longabaugh sisters is consistent with Mr. Long's claim that these are his sisters – the Longabaugh sisters. Equally clear is that Mr. Long is not a pseudonym for either of the McCarty's.

Suggested further work on identification would include DNA comparisons of known family members of Mr. Longabaugh with the samples extracted from Mr. Long, and facial reconstruction of the skull of Mr. Long. The usual practice of dentally-based identification is impossible.

Submitted by:

John M. McCullough, Ph. D.
Professor of Anthropology
University of Utah

Acknowledgements

I have gleaned helpful information and pictures for different parts of this book from the following authors, their published books, their stories, and their research and I am most thankful to them.

ANONYMOUS: I was provided with valuable information by a relative of an outlaw of the era who wants to remain anonymous.

BAKER, Pearl: Her book, *The Wild Bunch at Robbers Roost,* was her account of the stories she heard from some of the people that knew some of the outlaws that frequented the area and the Robbers Roost Ranch, which she owned.

BARTON, Doris: Was the first person to make the Ann Bassett Etta Place connection in her book, *Queen Ann Bassett, alias Etta Place*.

BURTON JEFFREY: His book, *The Deadliest Outlaws,* is the source I used for the Folsom New Mexico train robbery.

BETENSEN, Lula Parker: She put the many false records straight in her book, *Butch Cassidy, My Brother*; which puts Butch in his father's home seventeen years after he was Supposedly killed. Salute Lula!

CARSLON, Chip: His book, *Tom Horn: Blood on the Moon:* is he story of the hired killer Tom Horn.

COURESHAINE, Rocky: Director of the Crook County Museum of Sundance, Wyoming, far surpassed any expectations of Cooperation in his diligent research for critical Sundance evidence.

DAVIDSON, Dan: Was the Curator of the Museum of Northwest Colorado. The museum acquired the David Gillespie letters, which were the key to discovering that Butch and Sundance went to South America.

ERNST, Donna: Her book *Sundance, My Uncle*, has the Longabaugh family history and genealogy.

FRENCH, William: His book, *Recollections of a Western Ranchman*, is the only firsthand account of Butch Cassidy's time in New Mexico at the WS Ranch.

KELLY, Charles: His book, *The Outlaw Trail,* was probably responsible for creating the legend of Butch Cassidy. He gathered information from people who actually knew the outlaws.

MEADOWS, Anne: Her book, *Digging up Butch and Sundance,* covers Butch and Sundance's story in South America. She also found the Government records in Bolivia of the 1908 "deaths" of the San Vicente bandits.

McCLURE, Grace: Her book, *The Bassett Women,* highlights the story of the Bassett family in Brown's Park, Colorado.

PATTERSON, Richard: Butch Cassidy: A Biography, is a summary of different versions of the same events told by different people. He has the best account of the 1894 trial of Butch.

RAPPLEYE, Christine: Assistant Editor for the *Deseret News* of Salt Lake City, Utah. She graciously provided me with their 1976 interview with Lula Bentensen.

SIRINGO, Charles: Was a Pinkerton Detective who chased "the gang" across the American West. His book, *A Cowboy Detective*, gives his accounts of those chases.

SKOVLIN, Jon & Donna Mc DANIEL

SKOVLIN, Donna: Their book, *In Pursuit of the McCartys*, chronicles the outlaw McCarty boys and their family.

TAYLOR, Kelly: A cousin of mine from Fremont, Utah. He guided me around Wayne County to see the sites, including Robbers Roost. He also coordinated with other Utah relatives for the documentary film interviews, the exhumation, forensic and pathological tests, and the re-burial of Sundance.

WARNER, Matt: He was a convicted murder who also rode with Butch and assumingly Sundance. His book, *Last of the Bandit Riders,* gives information from his point of view. It wasn't published until after his death.

WARNNER, Joyce.

LACY Dr. Steve: Joyce was Matt Warner's daughter. She and Dr. Lacy updated his book, *Last of the Bandit Riders Revisited;* with new information.

Acknowledgements

I am very thankful to the above writers and other individuals for their contribution in helping me sift through the mountainous amount of false information so that I could find out about my great-grandfather, the Sundance Kid. Many cousins and relatives have relayed to me stories of Sundance, and I thank them all very much.

~ **Jerry Nickle**

Bibliography

Manuscript and Archival Collection

Anaconda Standard Newspaper; Anaconda Montana

Ann Bassett Letter; Museum of Northwest Colorado, (Craig)

Asotin County Tax Records; Asotin, Washington

Axford, Joseph "Mack"; *Around Western Campfires*, Tucson

(University of Arizona Press, 1969)

Blackburn, Elias, Journal, Utah State Historical Society Utah, Salt Lake City

Billings Gazette, Newspaper, Montana, Billings

Census Records; Federal and State, Ancestry.Com, Utah, Provo

Chapman, Arthur; "Butch Cassidy," Elks Magazine

Cochrane and Area Historical Society, Big Hill Country, Canada, Alberta 1977

Colorado Magazine, Ann Bassett Willis, "Queen Ann of Brown's Park," Colorado, Denver

Court Records; H Longabough, Canada, Calgary

Court Records, (Crook County) Wyoming, Sundance

Daily Huronite, Newspaper, South Dakota, Huron

Daily Yellowstone Journal; Montana, Miles City

Daley Tribune, Newspaper, Montana, Great Falls

Deseret News, Newspaper, Utah, Salt Lake City

Deseret Evening News, Newspaper, Utah, Salt Lake City

Eau Claire Leader, Wisconsin, Eau Claire

Gillespie, David; Letters and Memoirs, Museum of North West Colorado, Craig Colorado.

Gooldy, John F.; Unpublished memoirs, American Heritage Center, University of Wyoming, Laramie

Great Falls Daily Tribune, Newspaper, Montana, Great Falls

Hadsell Papers; Bob Lee Interview, Meschter Collection, Casper College, Wyoming, Casper

Johnson, Ebb; Unpublished memoirs, Glenbow Institute, Alberta, Calgary, Canada

Kelly, Vicky, Butch and the kid, Glenbow Magazine, Glenbow Institute, Canada, Calgary, 1970

Natrona County; Justice Court Records, Wyoming

Nebraska State Journal, Nebraska, Lincoln

Ogden Standard Examiner, Newspaper, Utah, Ogden

Bibliography

Pinkerton Detective Agency Archives; the Library of Congress, Washington, DC

Rawlins Journal, Newspaper, Wyoming, Rawlins

Rawlins Republican, Newspaper, Wyoming, Rawlins

Robison, Irvin; Unpublished Family Dairy, Utah, Duchesne

Salt Lake Herald Newspaper; Utah, Salt Lake City

San Francisco Call, Newspaper; California, San Francisco

Sllver State Newspaper; Nevada, Winnemucca

Steamboat Pilot Newspaper; Colorado, Steamboats Springs

Sundance Gazette, Newspaper, Wyoming, Sundance

Tiffany Records, Recelpt. New York, NY City

The Santa Fe New Mexican; Pasatiempo, Hideout in the Glla, New Mexico, Santa Fe May 2012

The Spearfish Weekly Register Newspaper; Wyoming, Spearfish

The Leadville Dailey and Evening Chronicle, Colorado, Leadville

The Miner, Newspaper, Wyoming, Rock Springs

Thomas, John B, Papers, of Suffolk Cattle Company, American Heritage Center, University of Wyoming, Laramie

Washington State Penitentiary, Nelson Long Prison Record, Washington, Walla Walla

Wayne County; Utah Land Records, Utah, Loa

Books

Baker, Pearl; *The Wild Bunch at Robbers Roost,* New York: Abelard-Schuman, 1971

Betenson, Lula Parker; Butch *Cassidy, My Brother,* Provo, Utah: Brigham Young University Press, 1975

Burroughs John Rolfe; Where *the Old West Stayed Young,* New York: Bonanza Books

Burton, Doris, K. Queen Ann Bassett Alias Etta Place, Vernal, Burton Enterprises, 1992

Burton, Jeffrey: *The Deadlest Outlaws,* Dallas Texas: University of North Texas Press,2012.

Carlson, Chip; *Tom Horn, Blood on the Moon Dark History of the Murderous Cattle Detective,* Wyoming: High Plains Press, 2001

Engebretson, Doug; *Empty Saddles, Forgotten Names,* Aberdeen, S.D., North Plains Press, 1982

Ernst, Donna B.; The *Sundance Kid, Oklahoma,* Oklahoma Press, Norman, 2009

French, Captain William; *Recollections of a Western Ranchman,* New Mexico, *1883-1899,* High-Lonesome Books, 1997

Frye, Elnora L.; *Atlas of Wyoming Outlaws at the Territorial Penitentiary*, Cheyenne, Wyoming: Pioneer Printing and Stationery, 1997

Garman, Mary; Harry Longabaugh, the Sundance Kid, the Early Years, 1867-1869: Wyoming, New Castle, 1977

Horan, James D.; *Desperate Men,* New York: G.P. Putnam's Sons, 1949

Kelly, Charles; *the Outlaw Trail, a History of Butch Cassidy & His Wild Bunch*, 2nd edition, Bison Books: University of Nebraska Press, 1996

McClure, Grace; *The Bassett Women,* Ohio: Swallow Press/Ohio University Press, 1985

Meadows, Anne; Digging Up Butch and Sundance, Nebraska: University of Nebraska Press, 1994

Morrell, Eldon; Ancestry and Descendants of William Wilson Morrell

Patterson, Richard; *Butch Cassidy, A Biography,* Nebraska, University of Nebraska Press, 1998

Selcer, Richard F.; *Hell's Half Acre,* Texas: Texas Christian University Press, 1991

Siringo, Charles A.; a Cowboy Detective, a True Story of twenty-two Years with a World-Famous Detective Agency, Chicago: W.B. Conkey, 1912. Reprint, Lincoln: University of Nebraska Press, 1988

Skovlin, Jon M. and Donna M.; In Pursuit of the McCartys, Oregon, Reflections Publishing Co, 2001

Snow, Anne; Rainbow Views, History of Wayne County, Utah, Art City Publishing Co. 1977

Warner, Matt; (as told to Murray E. King, Revisited by Joyce Warner and Dr, Steve Lacy) Utah: Big Moon Traders, 2000

Wells, Jerry and Samuel M. and Minnie Z. Lisonbee, XX, Provo, Brigham Young University